PLAY WITH ME

100 GROUP GAMES FOR SCHOOL, HOME, PARK

ABHIPSA PARIDA

Made with ❤ on the Notion Press Platform
www.notionpress.com

Dedicated to friends & family

Contents

Contents

Foreword

When we come across a child with a special need, the first thing that comes to our mind usually is - he/ she cannot talk or, is walking differently or, cannot communicate or, showing some inappropriate behaviour, etc. It's usually about some form of "signs/ symptoms/lacuna of some kind"...

But, can you think what happens to a parent when a child is diagnosed as a special need child?? It's really very tough not only for his/her parents but also for the whole family to first accept and then adjust according to the needs of the child. However, it is also true that

> *"EVERY CHILD IS A FLOWER AND ALL MAKES THIS WORLD A BEAUTIFUL GARDEN." A FLOWER DOES NOT THINK TO COMPETE WITH THE FLOWER NEXT TO IT. IT JUST BLOOMS IN ITS OWN TIME. Every child has its own hidden potential, so does a special need child. It's our responsibility to nurture that potential with love, care and most importantly with patience."*

We all know that various therapies are available for our special need children. But I want to take a pause here.... because therapy alone cannot help you and your child to cope up with the situation. Then the question is, WHAT CAN HELP US??

We all know the answer... yeah... you all are right! It's PLAYING...

PLAYING is very important at the early developmental stages. It not only helpful for development of cognitive ability also helpful in healthy emotional and physical development. We can say PLAY always working as a medicine for overall growth and development of a child.

For a normal child, playing is a spontaneous ability. This natural skill helps a child learn the most important life skills required to function efficiently in a society. But, when it comes to a child with special needs, in most cases playing ability is very low or even absent. Even for a normal child, if we don't give them ample time for play, it's detrimental to his/her physical, cognitive, emotional, & social skill development.

WHEN YOU SEE A SPECIAL CHILD IS NOT PLAYING, WE SHOULD NOT CONCLUDE THAT A SPECIAL CHILD CAN NOT PLAY OR HE/ SHE DOESN'T LIKE TO PLAY.. THE REAL FACT IS THAT "THEY DONT KNOW HOW TO PLAY".

So, it's our responsibility to make them play. But in reality, most of time parents or caregiver of a special child do not know how to make this work possible in an effective way.

HERE I AM HAPPY TO SHARE THAT, "PLAY WITH ME" IS A VERYHELPFUL HANDBOOK FOR ALL. This book comes along with 100 different games. All the games are simple and can be easily understood by all. These games are designed in such a way that it will be helpful to develop not only socialization skills but also develop confidence, & healthy emotions among the children. There is a good list of Group games in this book. These games are simple rule-based games which can be understood & followed easily. The author has mentioned in precise details in a simple language about the steps of each game & what benefits it provides for the children.

When a child plays in a group, he/she gets ample opportunity to develop qualities like leadership, tolerance toward others approach, responsibility and patience. Playing Group games is the best platform for developing socializing skills, problem solving ability and higher thinking processes among children. Group games helps the children become independent, confident and become more self-reliant. These games are easy to play in both outside and inside environments.

And If I want to say about the author, she is one of the best OCCUPATIONAL THERAPISTS specializing in PEDIATRICS in Odisha. This is her second book after **"BEING JOYFUL WITH AUTISM"**. Her first book, "BEING JOYFUL WITH AUTISM" is one of the best-selling books and appreciated by many parents and professionals. She was also awarded THE AUTHORITY AWARD by

"THE INSTITUTE OF HEALTH SCIENCE" for her excellent contribution in her field. She is **ABHIPSA PARIDA**,a person having passion about her work and profession.

My personal experience with her is both personal and professional. As a mother of a special kid, I personally know her and she is my child 's first therapist and at the same position till date. She has more than 7 years of experience. She is a blogger and a youtuber too. She is successfully running her own institution at Bhubaneswar. I would like to congratulate her for this one step forward journey and give my best wishes for her new book "**PLAY WITH ME**"

Author of foreword

Name- **Maitri Mamata Panda** (MAJMC, MBA, B. ED IN SPECIAL EDUCATION, M.ED (CONTINUE), YOUTUBER, BLOGGER)

MOTHER OF SPECIAL KID TURN TO FULL TIME SPECIAL EDUCATOR

Preface

While I was taking a class, I heard some people talking excitedly outside the room. I became curious & opened the door. One of my students, Kakul was standing at the door with a medal & a certificate. Her mom told me that, she had won the 1ˢᵗ prize in "Running Race in the annual sports competition" at her school & a certificate of "maximum participation award" for participating in all the events that took place in the Annual sports day.

I was exhilirated to hear this! It was a proud moment for me.....

I thought to myself, "playing in groups has brought tremendous changes in the children & this is the result of that!"

I am a pediatric occupational therapist who is working with children with special needs since the last 7 years! For children, PLAYING is a natural & necessary skill that helps develop valuable life skills & the confidence to function in everyday life effectively. PLAY is the essential skill to develop friendships, bonding, & socialization. But, for children with special needs, this essential skill doesn't often develop naturally for which they might have difficulty in developing these important life skills which are highly essential to manuever through their daily life confidently. That's why, although these children are very gifted in many ways, & **they do want to play, to mingle with others, to make friends, to interact, to socialize,** they don't understand "how to do so". This often hampers their self confidence & might make it difficult for them to enjoy with others & their peers.

So, what can we do about it ?

Since PLAYING is the basis for the development & strengthening of all these skills, for the past few weeks, we were conducting a number of group sessions for the kids.

The games were focused on development of different skills like- confidence, competitiveness, sharing, turn taking, understanding games with rules, enjoying playing with friends, bonding, listening skills, attentiveness, communication skills, and so much more....

I have seen tremendous changes in Kakul and many other children within a short amount of time in many areas....

Kakul, was able to participate without fear in all the games, could understand the rules of the games & even win competitive games among so many other kids! It was really amazing.

Playing in groups in an environment which is supportive, encouraging, and focuses on your abilities really helped these children to boost their confidence and they have started enjoying with friends, socializing with others and easily doing things they usually had difficulty doing! Participating in these group games has helped these children to shine like stars & has helped to bring their hidden potential to the spotlight.

In this book, I have mentioned a 100 different group games that are focused on developing some important life skills in children. These games can be practiced for children with special needs as well as for normal kids. They can be practiced in any setting - at home, or school or park or therapy sessions also.

The purpose of this book is to make Socialization FUN & therefore something that children are naturally interested to do rather than hard work or something they "have to do for the sake of pleasing their parents/teachers/society."

Not just for children with special needs, these games are absolutely appropriate & highly beneficial for normal children also. The games described focuses in enhancing all areas of development- be it physical, emotional, cognitive, or social skills. If practiced in schools, or at home, playing these games will definitely help them become more successful in everything they do, to become confident, helpful, appreciative, & sociable individuals.

You will also find variations for different settings & for different age groups. I hope the games & activities will help all of you as much as it has helped me.

Acknowledgements

I would like to express my heartfelt gratitude to my parents & my brother for their support & encouragement.

They have always taken a keen interest in my work & have been enthusiastic supporters for my work which keeps me going.

A very special thanks to my friend Bhushan who has guided me & inspired me throughout the journey from the start to the finish. His brilliant innovative ideas have really helped me to structure my book. He has been an inspiring friend who helps spark that ray of enthusiasm once again whenever I had fallen short of ideas.

A very special thanks to one of the most optimistic, enthusiastic, inspiring parents of a smart autistic kid- Mrs. Maitri Panda. She has been a great source of inspiration to me.

I am very thankful to my friends Dr.Monali Das & Dr.Swarna who have whole heartedly supported & helped me while we were practicing the activities given in this book with the students. This book would not have been completed without their help & support.

A very special thanks to my friend Dr.Nivedita Mishra who has been an enthusiastic supporter of my work.

I am really thankful to all my teachers, friends,colleagues,seniors & juniors all of whom have taught me some valuable lessons that I have been inspired to mention in this book.

Last but not the least, I would like to thank the amazing parents of my students & the beautiful, creative, fun-loving little genius kids who have inspired me to write on this subject in the first place. The ideas presented in this book are possible because of the experiences I had with all of you. I couldn't have done it without you.

I
Introduction

What are Social skills?

Social skills are the rules, customs, and abilities that guide our interactions with other people. They play an important role in establishing our relationships with the society. In general, people tend to "pick up" social skills in the same way they learn language skills: naturally and easily. We tend to observe & imitate the social skills from our parents, family, & friends. Over time we build a social "map" of how to in act in situations and with others.

Developing social skills is about being aware of how we communicate with others, the messages we send and how methods of communication can be improved to make the way we communicate more efficient and effective.

Development of social skills requires the development of many other skills like-

- The ability to observe how other people around you especially those who are close to you are behaving in different situations & with different people.
- The ability to imitate those actions & behaviors in certain situations.
- The ability to generalize the behaviour/actions in other similar situations.
- The ability to judge, to rationalize & act according to the demands of the situation.
- The ability to communicate verbally , or nonverbally your own thoughts & feelings.
- The ability to understand another's feelings & needs in a particular situation.
- The ability to share your thoughts & feelings in an appropriate way.
- The ability to understand different relationships & how to respond to different people.

Since "observation" , "imitation", & "expression" are vital to learning social skills, for people with autism it can be harder to learn and build up these skills, forcing them to guess what the social "map" should look like in different situations & places. Also, it's hard for them to understand that different places & situations demand a different kind of behaiour.

Social skills development for people with autism involves:

- Direct or explicit instruction and "teachable moments" with practice in realistic settings
- Focus on timing and attention
- Support for enhancing communication and sensory integration
- Learning behaviors that predict important social outcomes like friendship and happiness
- A way to build up cognitive and language skills

Typical social skill deficits include difficulty in:-

- Initiating interactions,
- Responding to the initiations of others,
- Maintaining eye contact,
- Sharing enjoyment,
- Reading the non-verbal cues of others, and
- Taking another person's perspective.

Weak social skills are commonly found in children diagnosed with **Attention-Deficit Hyperactivity Disorder (ADHD), Autism Spectrum Disorder (ASD), Non-verbal Learning Disability (NVLD), and Social Communication Disorder (SCD).**

What is Autism?

It is a neurodevelopmental disorder characterised by these 3 features:

- Difficulty in social interaction
- Difficulty in verbal & nonverbal communication
- Repetitive/restricted patterns of thoughts & behavior.

Autism comes under Autism spectrum disorder(ASD)- which is a spectrum that includes- Autism, Pervasive developmental disorders not otherwise specified, and Asperger's syndrome.

Children with Autism spectrum disorders have difficulties in sensory processing. Different areas of the brain are affected in these children which leads to sensory processing difficulties, hormonal imbalance, disturbances in brain electrophysiology, deficits in cognitive skills, communication skills, emotional regulation, altering arousal levels, etc.

Autism comes under a spectrum, which means each child is very different from another child. Each child is affected differently & the way one child interprets any particular sensation/stimulation might be very different from one another.

Yet, socialization with other people might be very difficult for most of the children with ASD.

How is development of socialization skills affected in Autism?

Many children and adults on the autism spectrum need help in learning how to act in different types of social situations. They often have the desire to interact with others, but may not know how to engage friends or may be overwhelmed by the idea of new experiences

According to the DSM 5 Autism Diagnostic criteria,

A. Persistent deficits in social communication and social interaction across multiple contexts, as manifested by the following, currently or by history (examples are illustrative, not

exhaustive, see text):

1. Deficits in social-emotional reciprocity, ranging, for example, from abnormal social approach and failure of normal back-and-forth conversation; to reduced sharing of interests, emotions, or affect; to failure to initiate or respond to social interactions.

1. Deficits in nonverbal communicative behaviors used for social interaction, ranging, for example, from poorly integrated verbal and nonverbal communication; to abnormalities in eye contact and body language or deficits in understanding and use of gestures; to a total lack of facial expressions and nonverbal communication.

3. Deficits in developing, maintaining, and understanding relationships, ranging, for example, from difficulties adjusting behavior to suit various social contexts; to difficulties in sharing imaginative play or in making friends; to absence of interest in peers.

Summarising the above, we can conclude that, since these children perceive their environment differently, & the way they try to communicate is different, they have a hard time connecting with others in a meaningful or effective way...

Just like a plant needs sunlight, water, soil & fertilizers to grow, a child needs a supportive, encouraging & loving environment where he/she is accepted & loved to grow.

Why is developing socialization skills important ?

For children with autism, establishing friendship skills is a therapeutic lesson as much as a life lesson. A simple friendship can **boost self-esteem and confidence, improve their ability to forge connections with others, reduce social anxieties, and help them feel more accepted by others.** In most cases, developing friendship with peers, is a skill that's difficult for them more than any other skills. Therefore, in this book, I have mentioned some easy games which can be beneficial to develop important life skills like friendship, socialisation skills, communication skills, etc.

Now, let's take a look at the "other side" of these beautiful children. Having worked with children with special needs since the last 7 years, *I haven't met anyone more awesome, more gifted, more loving, more sensitive, more focused(in the areas of their interest) than these beautiful children.*

> **"Just like a plant needs sunlight, water, soil & fertilizers to grow, a child needs a supportive, encouraging & loving environment where he/she is accepted & loved to grow."**

On the other hand, if a child is not accepted for who he is, or treated differently, or criticized often, reminded a hundred times in a day about "what he cannot do" especially in his early developmental years, he/she will loose confidence & interest easily. I will share a story that will illustrate the above message.

Leo, a student on the Autism Spectrum studies in Std-1. His exams were going on. It was a rhymes singing exam. The students were called one by one to the front & they had to sing a rhyme. Now, it was Leo's turn to go to the front of the class & sing the rhyme. He was feeling scared & was hesitant to go. He sat on his desk looking anxious. The environment was overwhelming to him. When the teacher called his name again, he just couldn't bring himself to get up & sing the rhyme. He just sat on his desk & started rocking as he was feeling anxious. The teacher came to him, smiled & said calmly, "You can do it. You have practiced well. You can do it." Just then, one of his friends said "Go Leo go". Then, all of his friends started encouraging him by clapping & saying- "Go Leo!". This brought a big smile to Leo's face. He was feeling relaxed & confident now.

He got up, walked to the front of the class & sang the whole rhyme confidently.

The whole class cheered for him!

There was a big smile on Leo's face as he finished singing the rhyme.

In this story, the support & encouragement that Leo got from his teachers & friends gave him the courage to perform in front of the class confidently with ease...

For Leo, singing a whole rhyme was difficult. Remembering & verbalising the words of the whole song while making the action movements simultaneously was a difficult task. On top of that, performing that activity infront of the whole class with where he receives a bombardment of various sensory information was not easy.

Still, he could participate & even complete an activity which was not so easy for him due to his supportive teacher & friends! Isn't it amazing ?

More importantly, due to this supportive environment, Leo is very much interested to go to school everyday, to play with his friends, to have fun with his friends, to interact & socialize with them.

"When someone gets more love & encouragement than criticism, they can do things easily way beyond their visible abilities..."

Why am I sharing this story in this context ?

Because, during my work period, many a times, I have heard this complaint, "my child doesn't want to socialize" or "my child doesn't interact with his peers." So, next time, you think your child is not interacting with his friends, asking yourself the following questions might help you to find out the reason & help out your child.

- "Is this environment supportive & encouraging for my child?"
- "Is he having Fun here?"
- "Can he/she connect easily with these children/people?"
- "Is this environment overwhelming for my child?"
- "Is he encouraged for his efforts mostly or criticized?"
- "Are these activities fun & easy for my child to participate in or difficult?"

For children, they learn to socialize, to communicate through play. That's because play is fun & children are intrinsically motivated to participate in play. Play is ESSENTIAL TO LEARNING any skill for children. The characteristics such as – **joy, meaning, active engagement, iteration, and social interaction** – is associated with brain processes involved in learning.

Research also indicates that*social play and exploration lead to neurogenesis – the birth of new brain cells – in the dentate gyrus, a part of the hippocampus that plays a key role in learning and memory*(Barros et al 2019).

Thus, play involving a group of kids where they enjoy participating in games is the best way to develop socialization skills in children & is vital for the physical, social & emotional well-being of a child.

Before going into the list of games & their benefits, let's understand why & how playing games is the best way to enhance the development of socialisation skills in children in the next chapter.

II

Importance of Group Play

Play is an essential part of learning not just academics, but the basic skills that we need to have in our everyday lives in order to live to the fullest of our abilities.

Through play, we learn how to

- Take our own decisions
- Believe in ourselves
- Communicate effectively
- Solve problems
- Taking care of our & other's needs
- Be creative

And so much more....

Play is the vehicle for learning, especially in early development, but actually throughout our lives.

There are different stages of play which develops according to the age of a child & there are various classifications about the different types of play. Here, we will be talking specifically about the significance of ***"Playing in groups"*** especially in the light of ***developing social skills*** in children. When we talk about social play, we speak of a process of moving from solitary play with objects, the body, and the environment, and expanding to parallel play, cooperative play, and collaborative play involving other people.

If you observe a group of small kids playing a game of "Doctor doctor", or role-playing their teacher, or mother, their interactions can be very amusing to watch!

You will be surprised at their creativity in making the stories, the words & phrases they are using, & the non-verbal expressions while they are enacting the role-play!

Play encourages the development of communication skills & socialization by:

- Exposing children to new vocabulary by the different scenarios which they play out.
- Helps them understand that using words/language skills are essential to put forward your view inorder to be heard & understood.
- Children learn about their likes and dislikes, their interests, and their abilities.
- Children learn how to communicate their needs with their friends & also learn to understand the needs of their friends.
- By re-enacting different scenarios, they develop social etiquettes & also learn how to solve problems in different scenarios.

Apart from those skills, playing in groups helps in the development of many other important life skills.

Benefits of Group games-

- Enhances development of communication skills
- Encourages making friends
- Teaches social skills like cooperation, sharing, helping others, assertiveness, waiting for turn, compassion, etc.
- Encourages working together with others
- Enhances learning about friendship, enjoying working together, respecting the opinions of themselves as well as others.
- Develops problem solving skills, leadership skills, imagination skills.
- Helps in developing self-confidence.
- Also enhances learning of social etiquettes, learning to work together with others, to inspire & encourage others when they are down.

I would share another story which exemplifies how group games help children in developing these skills.

It was a group session that day. There were three kids- Khush, Kakul & Shivya. They were playing "Run & Fix" game. In this game, there are equal number of puzzles placed at one end for each of the players & their respective puzzle boards at the other end of the room. They had to take one puzzle, run & fix it in its board. Whoever finishes all their puzzles first, wins the game. I explained the rules to all of them. They were very excited for the game. When the game started, they all started running with their puzzles. Since Kakul was playing that game for the first time with other kids, she had trouble understanding the rules of the game. Although she was running on my instructions, she was not fixing the puzzles. Since I was the only therapist giving instructions to everyone, Kakul could only fix 3-4 puzzle pieces.

In the meantime, Khush finished all his puzzles & won the game! He was very happy because he won the game. Just after that, Shivya also finished all her puzzles & was excited. Still, Kakul had a few puzzles left & she was somewhat confused about what to do. She stopped running...

Just then I asked Khush & Shivya, let's all clap for Kakul! So, we all started clapping for Kakul. She was excited again & one by one, she fixed all the remaining puzzles by running. We kept clapping until she was done.

In this small story, the kids not only learnt the concept of win/loose & competitiveness, but also to encourage & uplift their friends. Kakul was so happy when she was encouraged by her friends, she was re-excited, re-ignited to start running again to finish her puzzles.

This beautiful story is a great example of how playing in groups can teach kids to encourage each other, to help others, to uplift their friends, to value friendship alongwith sense of competitiveness, focus & sportsmanship.

In this book, I have talked about different group games which are easier to practice both for parents & therapists. You can choose from these group games which can be practiced according to the age & level of a child & which skill you want to develop in him/her. Different games focus on different skills, most importantly all of these games focus on developing important life skills of **bonding, socialization, friendship, & team work.**

These games will be highly beneficial to strengthen the skills already present in a child as well as to develop the skills that are not developed. Alongwith that, children will also learn to work together with other kids who-

- Are good at different things,
- Have different ways to do things &
- Have different things they enjoy

Primary Components focused upon in these activities are:-

- Enjoying with other children
- Communicating your needs

- Interacting with friends
- Responding to name call
- Following Commands
- Understanding & responding to your turn
- Imitation
- Working with others as a team
- Body Awareness
- Motor Planning
- Listening skills
- Visual Spatial Perception
- Coordinating Body sides
- Perception of Movement
- Perception of Touch
- Fine motor skills
- Cognitive skills
- Problem solving skills
- Communication skills
- Waiting for turn
- Concept of Winning/Loosing
- Helping others

Tips to help you and your child get the most out of group games:

? Encourage play in different environments.

For example, if your child likes playing ball games at home with you, encourage your child to play with ball at a friend's house or at a relative's house or at park with other kids. Reward him for playing and using his skills in different places and with different people.

? Follow your child's lead with play.

Encourage your child to lead the play while playing with his friends in your guidance. You can ask each of his friends to take turns to lead different games.

? Work with your child's learning strengths.

For example, if your child is a visual learner, you can work with this strength by using pictures of the different steps in a game or activity.

? Enjoying the process should be a priority

Make sure the children are enjoying the activity together. Enjoying the process should be more important than following the rules & completing an activity when you are playing in groups.

? Allow some time for free play without any rules.

Children are able to boadcast the most of their skills when they feel free & not restricted by rules. Allowing some free play where kids just run around giggling or just having fun in their own way is the best way for them to experience the fun of playing with friends. This might not seem meaningful to you, but it really provides the basis for that connection with other kids.

? Avoid giving any negative comments infront of his friends.

Giving negative feedback infront of others terribly hampers your child's self-esteem. So, avoid giving any criticizing or negative comments infront of his friends. Encouraging everyone not only boosts their self-esteem, but also teaches everyone how to uplift each other when someone is down.

Group play benefits children hugely in developing their self-esteem and self-awareness.

It also allows children to experience and express both positive and negative feelings. They learn how to modulate the effect of these emotions, how to deal with them positively, how to control their impulses, learn good manners and positive behaviour. They learn about their own response to various emotions & also about others.

I would share another story that exemplifies the importance of how playing in group helps children to connect with each other more, to communicate their needs & understand the needs of another & in forming a bond of friendship.

It was a group session that day in my clinic. There were 4 students in that session. As we began the session, I noticed that the usually happy & energetic kids seemed to be a little grouchy. So, I decided to begin with music games, followed by jumping games, & colouring games, to make them happy.

Yet, after two-three activities, they still didn't seem excited. There was still some grumpiness. I didn't want them to participate in the activities following the rules just for the sake of the class. But, I also didn't know how to cheer them up at that time. So, I called Gundu & asked her, "what happened Gundu?" Since she is almost always happy & excited for the classes, especially the group class, but that day, even she was not in her usual happy state. I gave her a hug. Just then, Shivi who was standing near Gundu, asked me, "What happened ma'am?" I said, "Gundu is sad. So, I giving her a hug to make her smile." Shivi came to us & gave a big hug to Gundu smiling. Seeing this, the other two kids, Khush & Kakul also hugged each other. Then, there was a big smile in everyone's faces. I was so happy that this little kid, Shivi could light up everyone that day. It was, as if by magic, everyone was rejuvenated, re-energized, & excited! After that, ALL the kids were very excited & happily participated in all the group activities. It was so much fun for me & them as well.

That experience was valuable for the kids as it gave them an opportunity to learn-

- To have fun with friends
- Forming bonds with friends
- Sharing their emotions
- Enjoying activities together
- Understanding each other's feelings & needs.
- Supporting & encouraging each other.

Most importantly, that day, since the kids started enjoying the session, even more they started enjoying each other's company....

III
Easy Socializing games

In this chapter, we will be talking about some simple games that focus primarily on -building friendships, & enhancing bonding with friends. Children enjoy all of these games, thus, making socialization easy & fun.

Easy Socializing games for young kids

Ringa Ringa Roses

Ringa Ringa Roses

This is a game most toddlers enjoy playing.

<u>Number of Participants</u> - 3 or more

<u>Equipment Required</u> – None

<u>How to play</u> -

All children hold hands, travel around in a circle, in either a clockwise or anti-clockwise direction, while singing the popular nursery rhyme- Ringa ringa roses & sit down at the end of the song with the words- "we all fall down."

<u>Benefits</u> -

This game helps in developing the following skills:

· Enjoying with friends

- Following the instructions of the game
- Body awareness required to keep holding their friend's hands while moving round & round
- Listening skills essential to "sit down" when the line comes- "We all Fall down"

London Bridge is Falling down

London Bridge is Falling down

<u>Number of Participants</u> - 3 or more
<u>Equipment Required</u> – None
<u>How to play</u> –

- Two kids stand facing each other holding hands at a height that other kids can pass through easily.
- The song- "London bridge is falling down" is played.
- Other students pass in between & around the two kids (who are holding hands).
- Each time this line in the song comes-"My fair lady", the kids holding hands catch the kid whoever passes in between them.
- Now, this kid (who is caught) holds hands with one of them while the other continues moving in between & around the kids holding hands.
- This game continues till each kid is "caught".

<u>Benefits</u> -
This game helps in developing the following skills:

- Enjoying with friends
- Waiting for Turn in a line
- Listening skills essential to "catch the friend" when the line comes- "My fair lady"
- Following the instructions of the game
- Planning to keep hands raised so that a friend can easily go through.

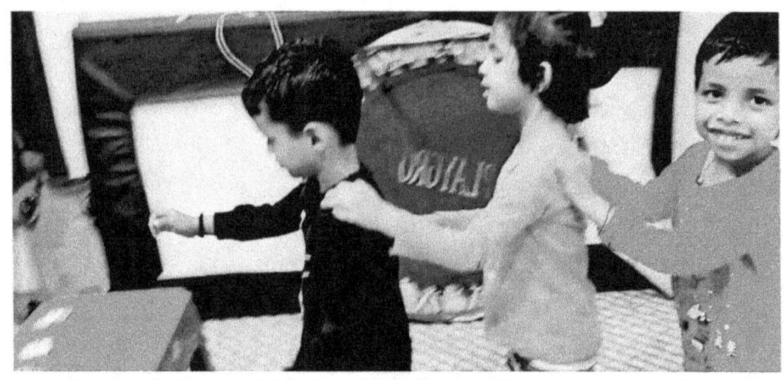

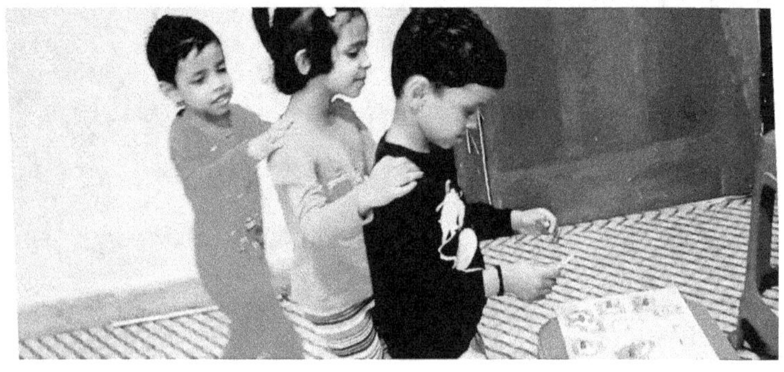

Chook Chook Train

Chook Chook Train

<u>Number of Participants</u> - 3 or more
<u>Equipment Required</u> – None
<u>How to play</u> –

- All the kids stand in a line. Each child stands at the back of a child holding his/her shoulders.
- They all stand holding the shoulders of the child in their front. The child at the front is the "Train Driver" who leads all of them.
- You can mark different spots as "Train stops", or "stations". You can either use any object like a large stool, or chair or a box or the door as "Station".
- Make a path for their train- It can be a straight path or with turns.
- When you say "start", the kids all walk in a line holding each other's shoulders with both hands making the "chook chook sound".
- When they arrive at a "Station", they change positions & another child comes to the front. They take turns to change positions at each "station".
- Make sure they hold the shoulders with both hands while the train is moving/taking a turn.

<u>Benefits</u> -
This game helps in developing the following skills:

- Enjoying with friends
- Waiting for Turn in a line
- Following the instructions of the game
- Body awareness required to keep holding their friend's shoulders while walking & taking turns
- Motor planning skills

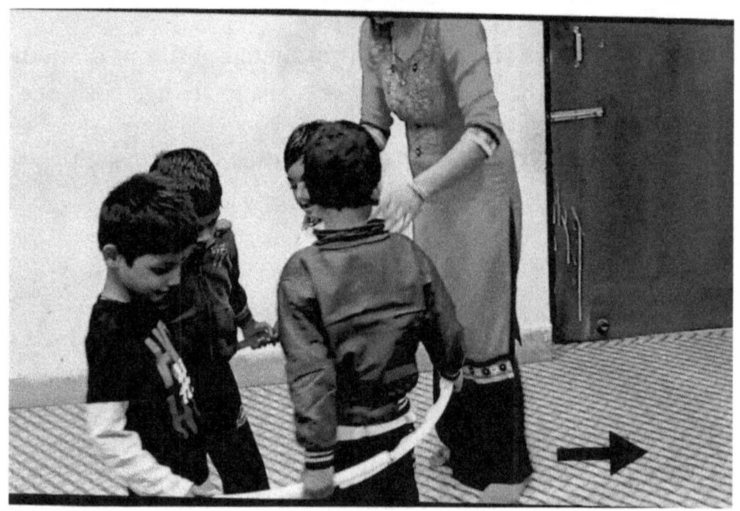

Walk inside a Ring

Walk inside a Ring

<u>Number of Participants</u> - 3 or more
   <u>Equipment Required</u> – A hoola hoop
   <u>How to play</u> –

- All children stand inside the hoola hoop holding it & walk together from one end of the room to the other end completing puzzles.
- Take turns to pick up the puzzle & fix it.
- Others should wait while one kid is fixing a puzzle.
- They all should hold the hoola hoop & start walking together to get the next puzzles until all the puzzles are completed.

<u>Benefits</u> -
This game helps in developing the following skills:

- Enjoying with friends
- Following the instructions of the game
- Body awareness required to keep holding the hoola hoop while walking & while fixing a puzzle
- Waiting for all friends to take puzzles/fix puzzles before beginning to walk
- Team work & cooperation
- Motor planning skills

Easy Get to know another games for young kids

Run Run Run & Touch

Run Run Run & Touch-

<u>Number of Participants</u> - 4 or more
<u>Equipment Required</u> – None
<u>How to play</u> –

- All the kids stand in a line at a little distance from one another.
- One child comes to the front.
- Teacher commands- "Run run run & touch Ayush". Then come back.
- Again, teacher commands- "Run run run & touch Sai." Then come back.
- Take turns to call each child.

<u>Variation for older children</u> –

- They can use different movements like- "Hop hop hop & touch",

"Bear walk & touch", "Bunny hop & touch" instead of run run run & touch.

<u>Benefits</u> -

This game helps in developing the following skills:

- Responding to one's name call
- Waiting for Turn
- Listening skills essential to respond only when "your name is called"
- Getting to know your friends' names.
- Motor planning required while performing the actions like "Bear wlk or Hopping,etc"

Pass the ball (on Name call)

Pass the ball (on Name call)-

Number of Participants - 4 or more

Equipment Required – A ball. (A football or a gymball or a softball can be used)

How to play –

- All the kids sit or stand in a line or forming a circle at a little distance from one another.
- One child comes to the front.
- Teacher commands- "Roll/throw the ball to Aadi".
- "Roll or throw the ball to Gundu".

- Take turns to call each child.
- Or, let them stand forming a circle at distance from one another.
- Ball is rolled to whosever name is called. Example- "Pass the ball to Kakul". Next, "pass the ball to "Sibya".

<u>Variation for older children</u> –

- They can be in standing position at a distance from one another
- The ball can be passed in one bounce, two bounce,etc.

<u>Benefits</u> -
This game helps in developing the following skills:

- Responding to one's name call
- Waiting for Turn
- Listening skills essential to catch the ball when "your name is called"
- Remembering your friends' names to pass the ball.
- Eye contact
- Impulse control- to stand still inside one's ring while the ball is passed between other friends

Who has the cup?

Who has the cup?

Number of Participants - 4 or more
Equipment Required –

- Different Coloured cups/stacking cups.
- Pom poms or colour beads

How to play –

- All the kids sit or stand in a line at a little distance from one another, each holding a cup of one colour.
- One child comes to the front. *Example-* Kakul comes to the front.
- Teacher gives a pom-pom to her & commands- "Give it to Sibya". Then come back.
- Teacher gives another pompom & commands- "Give it to Aadi". Then come back.
- Take turns to call each child. (Make sure he goes to the child with the same colour cup as the pom-pom he is holding).

Benefits –
This game helps in developing the following skills:

- Colour Matching
- Responding to Name call
- Listening skills
- Simple Communication skills
- Eye contact
- Remembering the names of friends

Clap on Name-call

Clap on Name-call-

<u>Number of Participants</u> - 3 or more
    <u>Equipment Required</u> – None
    <u>How to play</u> –

- All the kids stand/sit in a line at a little distance from one another.
- Teacher calls out the name of a student.
- Whosever name is called, claps.

<u>Variation</u> –

- They can use any other action to respond to their name like- Raise one hand, Nod your head, Raise two hands, Jump, etc.

<u>Benefits</u> –
This game helps in developing the following skills:

- Responding to one's name call
- Waiting for Turn
- Listening skills essential to respond only when "your name is called"
- Attention
- Following the instructions to respond with an action like "clap", or "raise hands",etc
- Getting to know your friends' names.

IV

Easy Communication Games

"Whenever children say "let's play pretend," a new landscape of possibilities for learning is revealed. When children pretend, they try on new feelings roles and ideas, they stretch their minds along with their imaginations.
Unknown"

As the name suggests, this chapter has a list of games that encourage interaction between friends. These games focus upon-

- Simple interactions,
- Communicating your needs,
- Asking questions,
- Answering questions,
- Building up language skills,

Thus, instilling confidence in children while enjoying an activity with friends.

ABHIPSA PARIDA

Easy Communication Games

Let's colour together

Let's colour together

This is an easy game that teaches asking for one's needs & saying thank you. It encourages basic communication while enjoying the colouring activity.

<u>Number of Participants</u> - 2 or more

<u>Equipment Required</u> –

- Similar pictures (one picture for each child)
- Colours (Crayons or sketch pens)

<u>How to play</u> –

- All children sit in a circle.
- Distribute colours among the students so that each gets one, or, two colour crayons/sketch pen.
- Whenever one student has finished using his colour, & needs a colour he doesn't have, he has to look for which friend has that colour he needs, & ask "Give me yellow".
- After getting the colour from his friend he can say "thank you".
- This game continues with students asking their friends for the colours they need until each one has completed their picture.

<u>Benefits</u> –

This game helps in developing the following skills:

- Enjoying an activity with friends
- Communicating to a friend when "you need a colour"
- Interacting with friends while colouring
- Waiting - when a friend is using a colour you need
- Colouring skills- Identifying which colours you need, Colouring within the lines, Using the right colour at the right place
- Fine motor skills

- Responding when someone is "asking You for a colour"
- Attention
- Waiting for friends to complete their work
- Appreciating your own & other's work
- Imitation skills

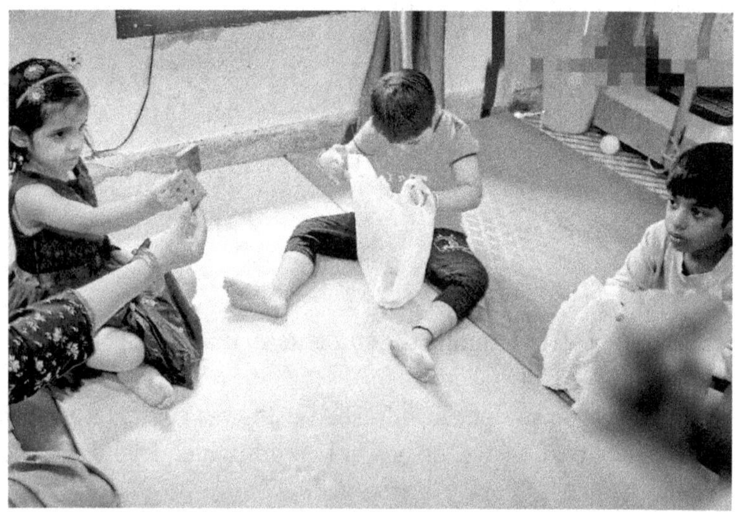

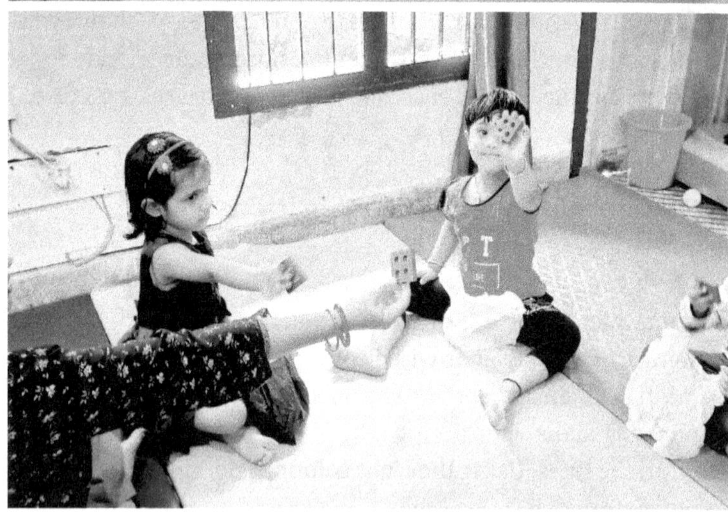

Who has?

Who has?

This game can be modified for older & younger kids.

Number of Participants - 3 or more

Equipment Required –

- A list with names or pictures of some common items (can be different in different settings & for different age groups)
- Bags to keep your items (one for each child)
- Alternatively puzzles can be used.

How to play –

- All students sit in a line with their bags.
- There is a list of items on a paper.
- Each child is given some items from the list INSIDE THEIR BAGS.
- The teacher calls one of the students to the front. He/she reads aloud the first item on the list & asks "Who has a yellow ping pong ball?"
- All the other students look inside their bags. Whoever has the item, raises his hand & says- "I have it".
- He gives it to the student at the front who matches the object with his items on the list.
- The game continues until all the items on that list are found.
- Next, the teacher can shuffle the items among the students & call the next student to the front.

To hide in the bags Items can be – a ping pong ball, a spoon, a small toy car, a pencil, a smiley ball, an eraser, a key, a fruit,etc)

Variation for younger kids-

- Some puzzles can be used for younger kids.
- The teacher can show them one square puzzle while asking "Who has Square?"
- The students start searching in their bags. Whoever has it, raises his hand & says "I have it".
- Then, one student comes to the front, & asks, "Who has circle?"
- Continue turnwise.

Benefits –
This game helps in developing the following skills:

- Enjoying an activity with friends
- Simple communication skills
- Skills of "Asking questions"
- Waiting - when a friend is using a colour you need
- Cognitive skills
- Attention
- Imitation skills
- Confidence

Who's puzzle is this

Who's puzzle is this

Number of Participants - 3 or more
   Equipment Required –

- Some category puzzles (one for each child)
- A tub/basket to keep the puzzles.

How to play –

- All students sit in a line with their puzzle boards.
- The teacher has all the puzzles in a basket.
- The teacher calls one of the students to the front, gives him a puzzle.
- The teacher then asks her, "Give it to Gundu."

- The student goes to Gundu & says "Gundu take Mango." Gundu replies "Thank you."
- Whosever name is called, goes to the teacher, takes a puzzle, goes to the respective student with that category puzzle & gives saying- "Take it".

Variation –

- The student who takes the puzzle can ask "Who needs Mango?"
- Whichever student has the fruit puzzle board raises his hand & says "I need Mango."
- The game continues as before.

Benefits –

This game helps in developing the following skills:

- Simple communication skills.
- Interaction with friends
- Waiting for your turn
- Eye Contact
- Responding when someone is "Giving you a puzzle"
- Asking simple questions
- Responding to simple questions like "Who needs Mango?"
- Attention
- Self confidence
- Imitation skills

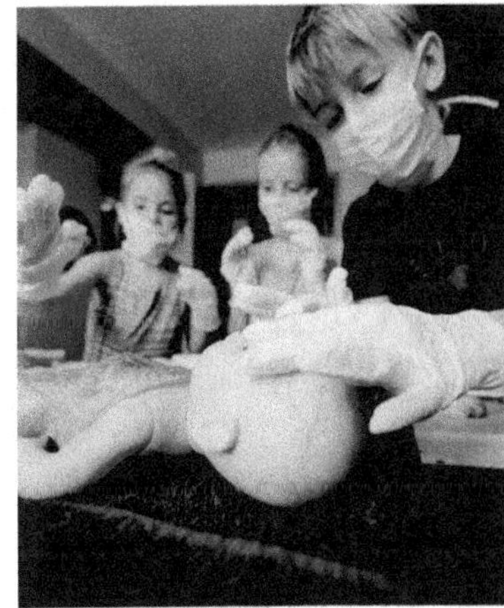

Role-Playing

Role-Playing-

This is an excellent game that enhances communication skills, builds up imagination, problem solving skills, team work, etc.

<u>Number of Participants</u> - 3 or more

<u>Equipment Required</u> – None

<u>How to play</u> –

- Make some teams & give any common scenario/roles that the students need to act out.
- They can decide who gets to act out which role.
- You can give any roles like-

  - *Students/Teacher*
  - *Shopkeeper/Customers*
  - *Doctor/Patient*

You can also give any scnenarios to act out like-

- *Suppose we are out at a restaurant with our family. Give roles of different family members & the server to the students*
- *When you are going out to watch a movie with your friends.*
- *A day at home during a holiday.*

<u>Benefits</u> –

This game helps in developing the following skills:

- Enjoying an activity with friends
- Simple communication skills.
- Vocabulary
- Interaction with friends
- Eye Contact
- Asking simple questions
- Responding to simple questions
- Imagination & creativity
- Team work & cooperation
- Understanding the various roles in a society

- Attention
- Self confidence
- Observation & Imitation skills

V
Turn-taking Games

These games mainly focus on som important skills like-

- Taking turns
- Waiting for your turn
- Responding to your turn
- Responding to your name
- Impulse control
- Attentiveness

Turn-taking Games

Fixing puzzles turnwise

Fixing puzzles turnwise

<u>Number of Participants</u> - 3 or more
  <u>Equipment Required</u> –

- Alphabet/Number puzzles

<u>How to play</u> –

- All children sit in a circle.
- You can use alphabet/number puzzles for this game. The puzzle board is placed at the center.
- To start, I will fix "A", next kid will fix "B", next will fix "C". Keep on fixing the letters sequentially taking turns till "Z".
- You can also use Number puzzles & the kids can fix sequentially. *Example*-Adnan fixes "1", Gundu fixes "2", Sibya fixes "3", again Adnan fixes "4".
- The game continues till all puzzles are completed

<u>Benefits</u> –
This activity helps in the development of the following skills:

- Enjoying an activity with friends
- Following the instructions of the game
- Waiting for your turn
- Learning the sequence of letters/numbers
- Identification of letters & numbers
- Paying attention when it's your turn to fix & which number you have to fix
- Fine motor skills
- Visual perception

Pick your object

Pick your object-

Number of Participants - 3 or more
   Equipment Required –

- Different category puzzle boards (one for each child)

  How to play –

- All children sit in a circle.

- Each child has a puzzle board of a different category.
- Teacher has a bucket of all puzzles mixed up.
- Teacher shows the bucket to each kid turn-wise.
- They pick an item which belongs to the puzzle board they have & fix.
- Game continues turn-wise till each one's puzzles are completed.

<u>Benefits</u> –
This activity helps in the development of the following skills:

- Enjoying an activity with friends
- Following the instructions of the game
- Waiting for your turn
- Identification of different categories like fruits/vegetables/animals,etc
- Paying attention when it's your turn to fix & which puzzle you have to fix
- Finding your own puzzles/objects
- Fine motor skills
- Visual perception

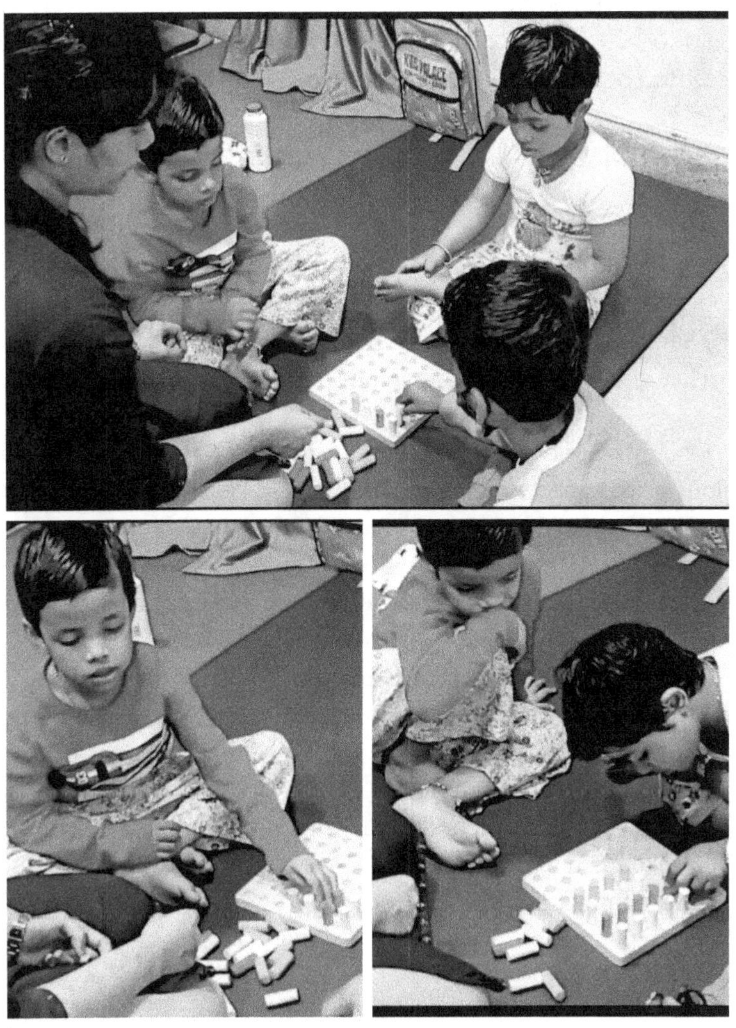

Pegboard game

Pegboard game-

<u>Number of Participants</u> - 3 or more
  <u>Equipment Required</u> –

- Different colour pegs & a pegboard

<u>How to play</u> –

- All children sit in a circle.
- Each child has to pick up a particular colour peg & fix on the pegboard.
- Then, the next kid picks up a peg & fixes it.
- They continue fixing their colour pegs turn-wise, in a row.

<u>Example</u>-Gundu fixes blue colour pegs, Kakul fixes Orange colour pegs, Adnan fixes yellow colour pegs. Pegs of the same colour must be fixed in a row.

  <u>Benefits</u> –
  This activity helps in the development of the following skills:

- Enjoying an activity with friends
- Following the instructions of the game
- Waiting for your turn
- Identification of colours
- Paying attention when it's your turn to fix & which colour you have to fix in which row
- Fine motor skills
- Visual perception

Threading beads turn-wise

Threading beads turn-wise

<u>Number of Participants</u> - 3 or more
   <u>Equipment Required</u> –

- Shape or colour beads
- Thread to string beads
- A Pattern of beads in a sequence

<u>How to play</u> –

- All children sit in a circle.
- One child picks up a bead matching the first bead in the pattern. *Example- Red circle*
- He threads the bead & gives the thread to the next child sitting beside him.
- Next kid picks up a bead matching the second bead in the pattern, threads it & passes the thread to the next child.
- Continue the game turn-wise.

<u>Benefits</u> –
This activity helps in the development of the following skills:

- Enjoying an activity with friends
- Following the instructions of the game
- Simple communication skills
- Waiting for your turn
- Learning to match different colour & shape beads with a pattern
- Identification of colours & shapes
- Sequencing skills
- Paying attention when it's your turn & which bead you have to thread
- Fine motor skills
- Visual perception

Hurdle crossing Game

Hurdle crossing Game-

<u>Number of Participants</u> - 3 or more
   <u>Equipment Required</u> –

- Any puzzle board
- Hurdles (Can be cylindrical bars, bolsters, floor ladder, boxes, training hurdles, or cones)

<u>How to play</u> –

- All children stand in a line.
- Arrange the hurdles from one end to the other end of the room.
- Put some puzzles at one end & the board at the other end.
- Each child picks up a puzzle, crosses the hurdles, fixes his puzzle on the board & comes back to the starting position.
- Then the next kid goes & repeats the same.
- All kids must wait in a line for their turn.
- Game continues till all the puzzles are completed

The hurdles can be given in different patterns using different objects to make it more challenging or easier for the kids.
   <u>Benefits</u> –
   This activity helps in the development of the following skills:

- Enjoying an activity with friends
- Following the instructions of the game
- Waiting for your turn in a line
- Body awareness
- Motor planning skills

Count in a sequence

Count in a sequence-

Number of Participants - 3 or more
   Equipment Required – None
   How to play –

- All the kids sit/stand forming a circle.
- The teacher stands in the front & starts by saying "1". First child says "2", Next says "2".
- You can continue till 20 0r 30. Then, you can start by counting backwards.

Variation-

- You can also skip count instead of counting serially. Example- Skip by "5's", Skip by "10's", etc.

<u>Benefits</u> –

This activity helps in the development of the following skills:

- Following the instructions of the game
- Waiting for your turn
- Learning the sequence of numbers
- Attention
- Listening skills
- Maths
- Counting forward & backward

VI

Impulse control Games

These are some simple & fun games for both younger & older children to teach impulse control which is a very essential skill to learn. This skill is very necessary for safety, discipline, following rules at school, home, & helps prevent chaos.

Run Run Run Stop

Run Run Run Stop-

This game can be played by younger kids. It's a simple & fun game to teach impulse control which is a very essential skill to learn.

Needs a large space for practice.

Number of Participants - 3 or more

Equipment Required – None

How to play –

- All the kids stand in a line at a little distance from one another.
- Teacher stands at the front with a whistle. When teacher says "Go", all kids start running towards the teacher.
- When teacher blows whistle & says "Stop", everyone has to stop.
- They can't move unless teacher again says "Go".
- You can say "Go" & "Stop", at different intervals. It requires some practice for younger kids to "Stop", whenever the whistle is blown.
- After some practice, you can simply say "Stop", without the whistle & everyone has to stop at that place.

Benefits –

This game helps in developing the following skills:

- Listening skills essential to "start" running & to "stop"
- Impulse control- to stop running when the teacher has told "stop"
- Waiting- for teacher to say "start" before you start running
- Motor planning skills

Red light & Green light-

This game can be played by older kids & pre-schoolers.

Needs a large space for practice.

<u>Number of Participants</u> - 3 or more
<u>Equipment Required</u> –

- A sign board made of paper attached to a stick/pen/cardboard as handle.
- There's a Red circle on one side & Green circle on the other side. It should be large enough for the students to notice from a distance while running.

<u>How to play</u> –

- All the kids stand in a line at a little distance from one another.
- Teacher stands at the front with the paper sign board. When teacher shows the "Green light", all kids start running towards the teacher.
- When teacher shows the "Red light", everyone has to stop.
- They can't move unless teacher again shows the "Green light".
- You can show "Red light" & "Green light", at different intervals.

<u>Benefits</u> –
This game helps in developing the following skills:

- Cognitive skills to understand the rules of the game
- Impulse control- to stop running when the teacher has shown the"red light"
- Waiting- for teacher to show "green light" before you start running
- Motor planning skills
- Balance & coordination

Ring ring ring Statue

Ring ring ring Statue-

This game can be played by older kids & pre-schoolers.

<u>Number of Participants</u> - 3 or more

<u>Equipment Required</u> – None

<u>How to play</u> –

- All the kids stand in a large circle.
- Teacher stands at the front & says- "Ring ring ring Statue!"
- When teacher says "Ring ring ring", everyone has to move/walk in a circle. You can use a hoola hoop as the demarcation of "a circle". The students can move around the hoola hoop.
- To make the game more interesting, you can choose any other action instead of walking like- hopping or jogging dancing inside the circle.
- Whenever the teacher says "Statue"- everyone has to stop.
- They can't move unless teacher again says "Ring ring" again.
- Whoever moves after the teacher said "statue", is out of the game.
- The game continues until there's one player left- who is declared as the winner.

You can play this game without the concept of win/loose.

<u>Benefits</u> –

This game helps in developing the following skills:

- Enjoying the game with friends
- Cognitive skills to understand the rules of the game
- Impulse control- to stop moving when the teacher says "statue"
- Waiting- for teacher to say "Ring ring ring" before you start moving
- Concept of win/loose
- Motor planning skills
- Balance & coordination
- Observation & imitation skills

Freeze Game

Freeze Game

This game is similar to the previous game except you can play music instead of saying "ring ring statue"
Equipment Required – None
How to play –

- All the kids stand in a large circle at a distance from one another.
- When music starts to play, everyone has to move in a circle.
- Whenever the music stops, everyone has to stop.
- They can't move until the music is played again.
- Whoever moves after the music stops, is out of the game.
- The game continues until there's one player left- who is declared as the winner.

<u>Benefits</u> –

This game helps in developing the following skills:

- Enjoying the game with friends
- Cognitive skills to understand the rules of the game
- Impulse control- to stop moving when the music stops
- Waiting- for the music to start again before you start moving
- Listening skills
- Concept of win/loose
- Motor planning skills
- Balance & coordination
- Observation & imitation skills

VII
Action Imitation Games

Action Imitation Games

These games have numerous benefits & can be used for both younger & older kids in any setting- be it home, or park or school.

Follow the Leader

Follow the Leader-

<u>Number of Participants</u> - 3 or more
   <u>Equipment Required</u> – None
   <u>How to play</u> –

- All the kids stand in a line at a little distance from one another.
- Teacher(leader) stands at the front & makes some simple actions/movements like- Raising both hands up, marching, stand on your toes, bending down, clapping, jumping jacks, etc.
- All the students copy the teacher's actions.
- You can choose the action/movements making it simpler or a little difficult depending on the age of the children.

<u>Variation for older kids</u> –

- Call a student to the front & ask him to do some movements.
- All other kids can copy the movements of their "leader".
- Take turns to call each child to become the "leader".

<u>Benefits</u> –
This activity helps in the development of the following skills:

- Enjoying an activity with friends
- Following the movements of the teacher or student
- Body awareness
- Motor planning skills
- Use of both hands & legs at the same time
- Observation & Imitation skills
- Confidence
- Attention

Action with Rhymes

Action with Rhymes-

This is an excellent action imitation game for younger kids. It's easy & very enjoyable.

<u>Number of Participants</u> - 3 or more

<u>Equipment Required</u> – Phone or TV

<u>How to play</u> –

- All the kids stand in a line at a little distance from one another.
- Any popular action rhymes is played using phone. Rhymes can be- "Listen to the music," or "Teddy bear teddy bear," or, "Head shoulders knees & toes", or, "If you're happy & you know it", or any other rhymes that involves some actions/movements.
- Teacher(leader) stands at the front & makes the actions/ movements according to the lyrics of the rhymes.
- All the students copy the teacher's actions.

<u>Variation for pre-schoolers kids</u> –

- Call a student to the front & ask him to do the movements according to the words of the rhymes.
- All other kids can copy the movements of their "leader".
- Take turns to call each child to become the "leader".
- When practiced, all children can do the actions by listening to the words when the rhymes is played without following the leader.

<u>Benefits</u> –

This activity helps in the development of the following skills:

- Enjoying with friends
- Following the movements of the teacher or student
- Body awareness
- Motor planning skills
- Use of both hands & legs at the same time
- Observation & Imitation skills

- Auditory processing skills (Listening to words & doing the action)
- Attention

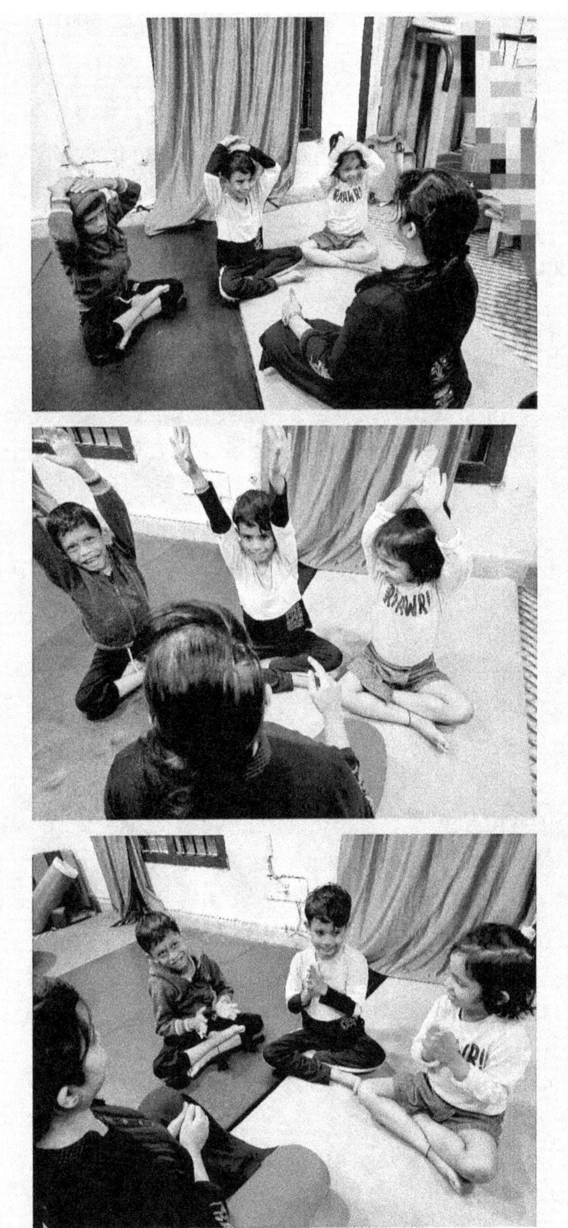

Verbal Imitations

Verbal Imitations-

This is another excellent action imitation game for younger & older kids. This is just like the above two activities except that the kids have to do an action by "listening only" not by "seeing".
<u>Number of Participants</u> - 3 or more
<u>Equipment Required</u> – None
<u>How to play</u> –

- All the kids stand in a line at a little distance from one another.
- Teacher says out loud any simple action & all the students have to do that action.

<u>Example</u>-Teacher can say "Touch your head", "Hold your ears", "Raise your hands"
"Turn around", "Clap your hands", etc.

- For older children, increase the complexity of actions & change commands quickly.

<u>Example</u>-Teacher can say "Touch your nose with your right hand", "Hold your right ear with left hand", "Touch your left knee with your right hand"
"Do 5 jumping jacks", "Clap your hands 3 times", etc.
<u>Benefits</u> –
This activity helps in the development of the following skills:

- Body awareness
- Motor planning skills
- Use of both hands & legs at the same time
- Observation & Imitation skills
- Auditory processing skills (Listening to words & doing the action)

- Multi sensory processing skills
- Paying attention to a new command & responding to it
- Attention

Simon says- "Raise your hands"

Simon Says -

This is a popular action imitation game for older kids. It requires a lot of focus

Number of Participants - 3 or more
Equipment Required – None
How to play –

- All the kids stand in a line at a little distance from one another.

- Teacher says out loud any simple action & all the students have to do that action.

- Rule is- Whenever teacher says "Simon says before an action"- *the students perform the action,* whenever the teacher says- "the action only"- *the students stand still with no action.*

- *If a student performs an action when the teacher hasn't said- "simon says before the action", he/she is disqualified.*

<u>Example</u>-Teacher can say "Simon says Raise your hands"- All students touch their heads, Next, Teacher says "Raise your hands"- All students stand still without performing any action.

Say different actions randomly saying "Simon says" before some actions & saying the actions without the words"Simon says". The students need to be very attentive to be able to get it correctly.

<u>Benefits</u> –

This activity helps in the development of the following skills:

- Enjoying the activity with friends
- Following the instructions of the game
- Understanding games with rules
- Body awareness
- Motor planning skills
- Observation & Imitation skills
- Auditory processing skills (Listening, & deciding when to do an action & when not to)
- Paying attention to a new command & responding to it
- Attention

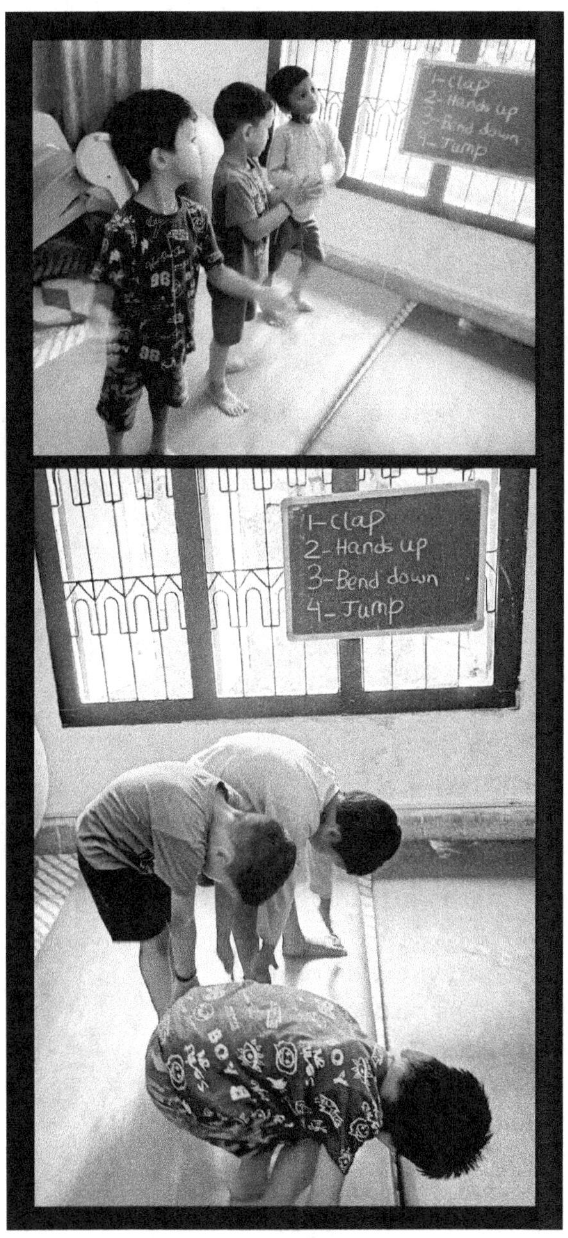

Read & Act

Read & Act-

This is another excellent action imitation game for older kids.
Number of Participants - 3 or more
Equipment Required – Blackboard/white board
How to play –

- All the kids stand in a line at a little distance from one another.

- Teacher writes some simple actions next to a Number/Alphabet

- When the teacher says a number, all the students have to do that action written next to that number.

*Example-*Teacher can write

1. "Jump 3 times",
2. "Clap your hands ",
3. "Raise your hands"
4. "Bend down"

Benefits –
This activity helps in the development of the following skills:

- Enjoying the activity with friends
- Following the instructions of the game
- Understanding games with rules
- Body awareness
- Motor planning skills
- Observation & Imitation skills
- Reading, understanding & executing an action
- Paying attention to a new command & responding to it

- Cognitive skills- to understand "the number of times" as well as "the action to perform"

VIII

Simple Win/Loose Games

Simple Win/Loose Games

These games can be used to teach the concept of winning/loosing.

These games are can also be given to young children/pre-schoolers. You can increase/decrease the level of difficulty according to the level of your child.

Make sure to use a reinforcement as a reward for winning a game. Reward can be anything simple like- a chocolate, a cookie, points, or a Star.

Using rewards makes it more interesting & kids are eager to participate with more dedication to win the game.

Threading beads competition

Threading beads Competition

<u>Number of Participants</u> - 2 or more
   <u>Equipment Required</u> –

- Shape or colour beads
- Threads to string beads (one for each player)

<u>How to play</u> –

- All children sit in a line.
- Each child is given 10 beads & a thread.
- When teacher says "Start", all kids start threading their beads.
- Whoever finishes threading 10 beads first, wins the game.
- The winner gets a small reward.

<u>Variation-</u>

- Instead of threading beads, you can also use anything else like colour pegs & pegboards (one for each participant), Or, putting coins inside connect 4 (one for each participant).
- Give equal number of coins/pegs to each participant.
- Whoever finishes putting pegs in pegboard, or putting coins inside connect 4 slots, wins & gets a reward.

<u>Benefits-</u>
This activity helps in the development of the following skills:

- Enjoying the activity with friends
- Following the instructions of the game
- Understanding games with rules- "Reward will be given to the student who completes all the beads first"
- Competitiveness
- Concept of win/loose
- Concept of completing an activity quickly
- Fine motor skills

Fixing puzzles Competition

Fixing puzzles Competition

You can choose the puzzle according to age & level of child.

Example- Choose any category puzzle board with large puzzle pieces for younger children & any picture puzzle with smaller pieces for older children.

Number of Participants - 2 or more

Equipment Required –

- Any puzzle boards (one for each player)
- Each puzzle board should have equal number of puzzles.

How to <u>play</u> –

- All children sit in a line.
- Each child is given equal number of puzzle pieces & a puzzle board.
- When teacher says "Start", all kids start fixing their puzzles.
- Whichever child finishes fixing their puzzles first, wins the game.
- Give a small reward to the winner.

<u>Benefits</u> –
This activity helps in the development of the following skills:

- Enjoying the activity with friends
- Following the instructions of the game
- Understanding games with rules- "Reward will be given to the student who completes all the puzzles first"
- Competitiveness
- Concept of win/loose
- Concept of completing an activity quickly
- Cognitive skills- to fix one's own puzzles
- Fine motor skills
- Visual perception

Run & Fix Game

Run & Fix Game-

This is similar to the above game, except that the participants have to run to the puzzle board & fix the puzzles.

You can choose the puzzle according to age & level of child.

Example- Choose any category puzzle board with large puzzle pieces for younger children & any picture puzzle with smaller pieces for older children.

<u>Number of Participants</u> - 2 or more

<u>Equipment Required</u> –

- Any puzzle boards (one for each player)
- Each puzzle board should have equal number of puzzles.

<u>How to play</u> –

- All children stand in a line at a little distance from each other.
- Each child is given equal number of puzzle pieces & a puzzle board.
- Place the puzzles at one end & the puzzle boards at one end of the room.
- When teacher says "Start", each child takes one puzzle & starts running to his/her puzzle board.
- He/she fixes a puzzle, runs back & gets another puzzle.
- Whichever child finishes fixing their puzzles first, wins the game.
- Give a small reward to the winner.

<u>Variation</u>-

Instead of "run & fix", you can use any other movement/animal walk like- "Bearwalk & fix puzzles", or "Crabwalk & fix puzzles, or, "Bunny hops & fix puzzles", etc.

It will be fun & challenging to the kids.

<u>Benefits</u> –

This activity helps in the development of the following skills:

- Enjoying the activity with friends
- Following the instructions of the game
- Understanding games with rules- "Reward will be given to the student who completes all the puzzles first"
- Competitiveness
- Concept of win/loose

- Concept of completing an activity quickly
- Motor planning- to run in one's own lane maintaining balance
- Cognitive skills- to fix one's own puzzles

Hurdle crossing

Hurdle crossing Game-

This is similar to the above game, except that the participants have to cross hurdles to reach the puzzle board & fix the puzzles.

This game can be played in a large space area like a school playground for more participants.

You can choose the puzzle according to age & level of child.

Number of Participants – 2 or more

Equipment Required –

- Any puzzle boards (one for each child)
- Hurdles (Can be cylindrical bars, bolsters, boxes, training hurdles, or cones)

How to play –

- All children stand in a line at a distance from one another near their respective puzzles.
- Each child has a separate hurdle crossing path. The hurdles are placed at the same distance for each participant.
- Arrange the hurdles from one end to the other end of the room.
- Put some puzzles at one end & the board at the other end.
- Each child picks up a puzzle, crosses the hurdles, fixes his puzzle on the board & comes back to the starting position.
- Then takes another puzzle & repeats the same process.
- Whichever child finishes fixing their puzzles first, wins the game.
- Give a reward to the winner.

Variation for older kids-

- Instead of "fixing puzzles", you can make it complex by giving a small maths problem to solve at the end of the hurdles.

- You can also increase the complexity of the hurdles by adding more activities like- walking along a narrow path, or animal walks, or any other variety of movements along with crossing hurdles.

Benefits –

This activity helps in the development of the following skills:

- Enjoying the activity with friends
- Following the instructions of the game
- Understanding games with rules- "Reward will be given to the student who completes all the puzzles first"
- Competitiveness
- Concept of win/loose
- Concept of completing an activity quickly
- Body awareness
- Motor planning skills to cross hurdles quickly maintaining balance, or to perform an animal walk
- Problem solving skills

It was a group class that day. There were 5 students. We started with "Threading beads competition'. The purpose was to teach the concept of competitiveness & giving our best efforts to the work we do.

As the game started, although the kids were threading beads, there was a lack of competitiveness that should be there in a competition. Finally, Gugul finished threading all his beads first & became the winner. Still, there was no "winning happiness" on his face. I understood that to learn the concept of win/loose & competitiveness, I need to reward them as a reinforcemrnt. I gave him a chocolate as the prize for winning the game. He was very happy. The other students now were more interested to win!

So, we conducted another competitive game. It was- "Run & Fix". I could see the renewed interest of all the students now. This time, Paridhi ran fast enthusiastically & gave her full efforts. Finally, Paridhi won that game. This time, she knew she was the winner & asked me for the chocolate as her prize!

The students then learned the concept of win/loose & competitiveness due to the reinforcements! That day we conducted many competitive games & different kids won different rounds. They gave their best efforts in all the games that day. I was very happy that a small reinforcement worked like a magic to teach these kids the important concepts of - working with dedication & giving your best efforts to complete a work.

IX

Dice Games

These are some interesting rule based games for older children that focus upon-

- Developing sportsmanship
- Cognitive skills
- Attention
- Simple maths
- Enjoying games with rules
- Concept of win/loose
- Competitiveness

When children start enjoying playing games together, they start enjoying making friends, it builds up their self confidence, bonding with friends alongwith understanding of playing games with rules.

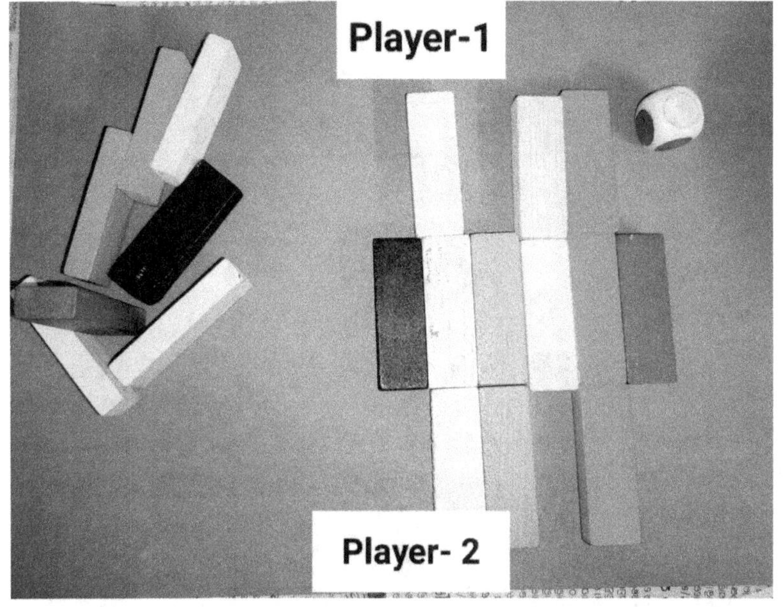

Dice game of Colours

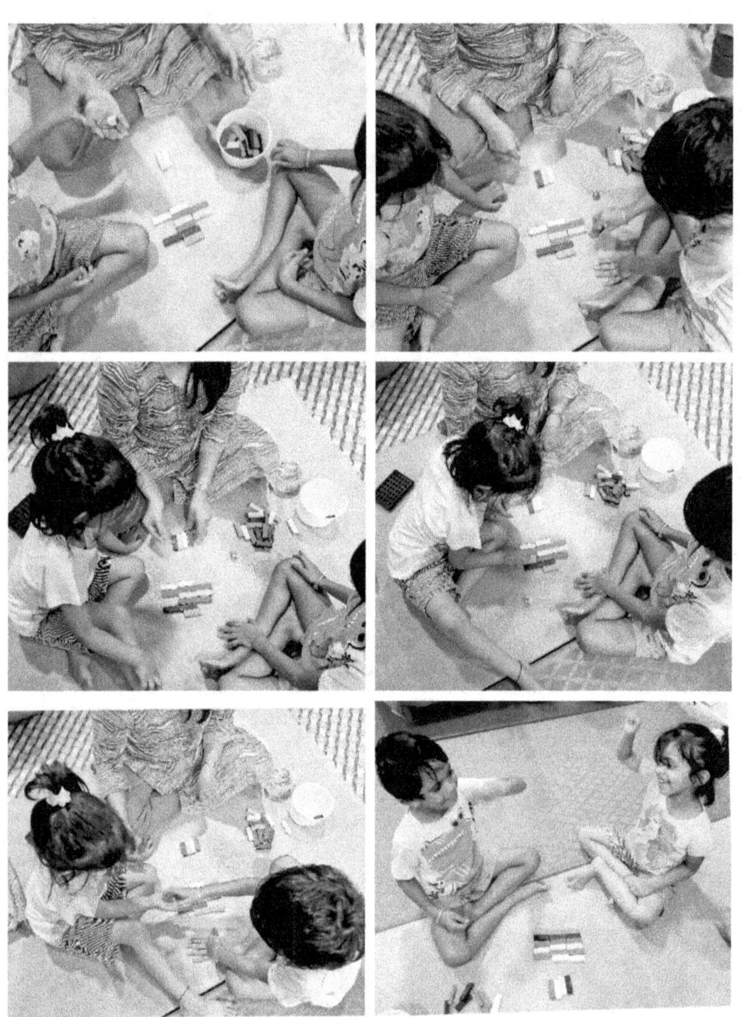

Dice Game of Colours

Dice Game of Colours-

This game can be used for older children.

<u>Number of Participants</u> - 2 or more

<u>Equipment Required</u> –

- Colour blocks
- Colour dice with one colour on each side of the dice

<u>How to play</u> –

- Sit in a circle.
- One player rolls the dice. Whichever colour comes, he has to pick the same colour block & pass the dice to the next player.
- Rule is- If you get a colour you already have, you don't pick the colour block, pass it to the next player.
- Whichever player gets all the 6 colours first, wins the game.
- The winner gets a reward.

<u>Benefits</u> –

This activity helps in the development of the following skills:

- Excitement of playing game with friends
- Interaction with friends
- Understanding games with rules
- Competitiveness
- Concept of win/loose
- Cognitive skills
- Colour matching skills
- Sportsmanship- accepting winning & loosing both as part of a game

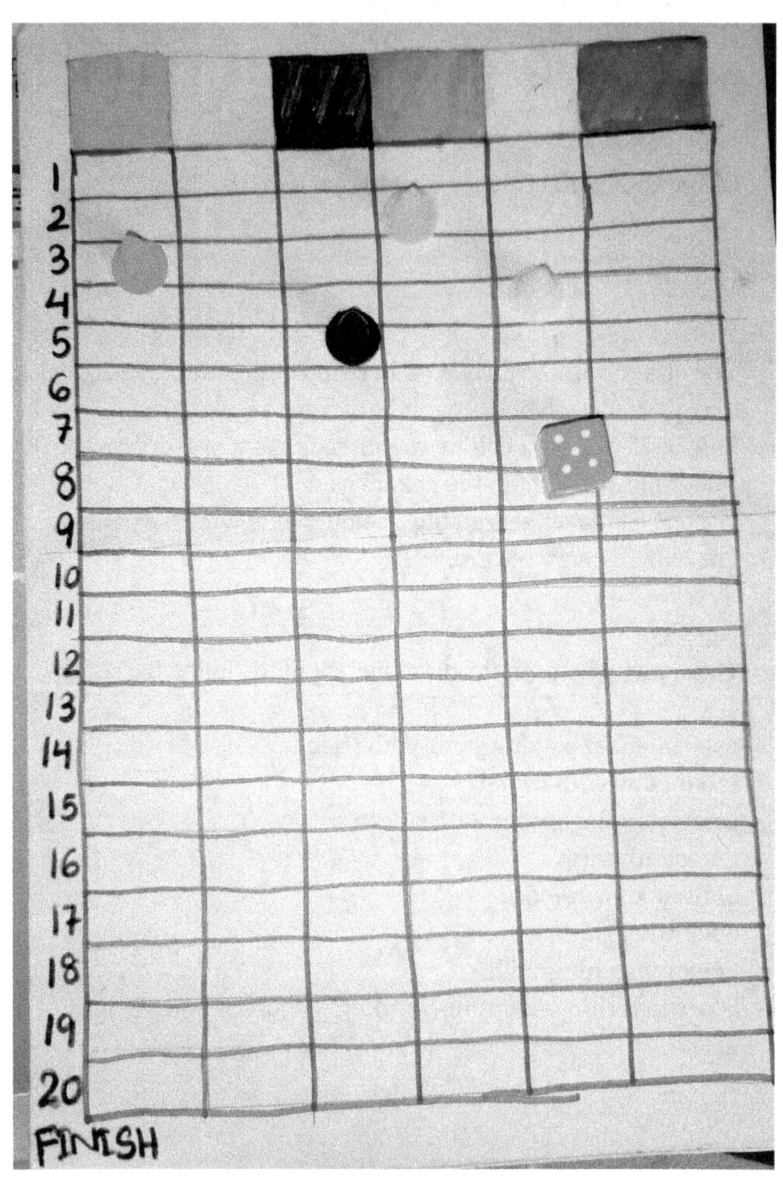

Dice Game of Numbers

Dice Game of Numbers-

This game can be used for older children.

Number of Participants - 2 or more

Equipment Required –

- Number board or Numbers 1-20 written on a paper with about 40 or more boxes drawn. *(Number of boxes = Number of players x 20)*
- Number dice/Ludo dice.
- Colour pegs/Ludo coins

How to play –

- Sit in a circle.
- Each player has a different colour peg/coin which is placed in a different row.
- As the game begins, each player must move his peg in his row of numbers till he reaches the last number (**20**).
- One player rolls the dice. Whichever number comes, he has to place his colour peg on that number & pass the dice to the next player.
- Roll the dice again & move forward along your row adding up the number you have got & pass the dice to the next player.
- Whichever player reaches the number 20 first, wins the game.
- The winner gets a reward.

Benefits –

This activity helps in the development of the following skills:

- Excitement of playing game with friends
- Interaction with friends

- Understanding games with rules
- Competitiveness
- Concept of win/loose
- Cognitive skills
- Visual perception to move your own colour peg along your row
- Math skills- simple addition
- Sportsmanship- accepting winning & loosing both as part of a game

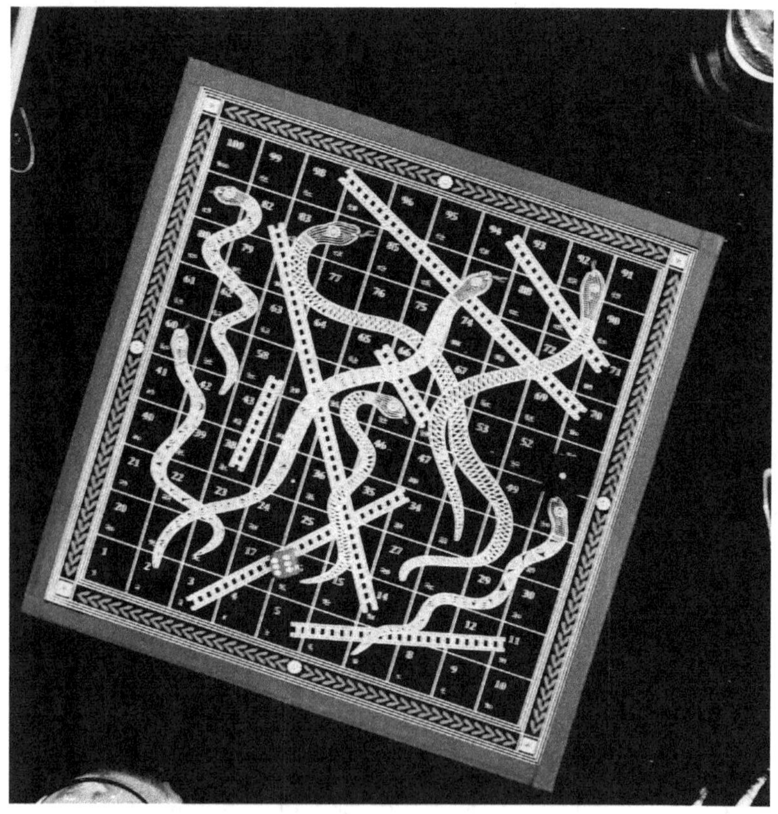

Ludo game of Snake/ladder

Ludo game of Snake/ladder-

This game can be used for older children.

    <u>Number of Participants</u> - 2 or more

    <u>Equipment Required</u> –

- Ludo dice.
- Ludo board of Snake/Ladder
- Colour pegs/Ludo coins

<u>How to play</u> –

- Sit in a circle.
- Each player has a different colour peg/coin. Start by rolling the dice.
- Play according to the classic snake/ladder rule. Climbing up when you reach a ladder & coming down when you reach a snake.
- The player to reach 100 first, wins.
- The winner gets a reward.

<u>Benefits</u> –

This activity helps in the development of the following skills:

- Excitement of playing game with friends
- Interaction with friends
- Understanding games with rules
- Competitiveness
- Concept of win/loose
- Cognitive skills
- Sportsmanship- accepting winning & loosing both as part of a game

Action with Numbers- using dice

Action with Numbers-

Number of Participants - 3 or more
   Equipment Required –

- Dice
- Blackboard/whiteboard

<u>How to play</u> –

- All the kids stand in a line at a little distance from one another.
- Teacher writes down the numbers 1-6 on the blackboard & some simple actions/movements on the board next to each number like-

- ***1)-Raise both hands up,***
- ***2)-March at a place,***
- ***3)-Bend down,***
- ***4)-Jumping jacks,***
- ***5)-Clap your hands,***
- ***6)-Turn around, etc.***

- The first student rolls the dice. Whichever number comes, he has to perform the action next to that number. Then, pass the dice to the next kid.

You can choose the action/movements making it simpler or a little difficult depending on the age of the children.

- *Example-* For Older kids, you can add the number of times they have to perform an action. Like-

  - ***1)- 10 jumping jacks***
  - ***2)- 5 Sit-ups***
  - ***3)- 10 Cross-crawls***
  - ***4)- 5 Squat jumps***
  - ***5)- 10 Claps***
  - ***6)- 5 Mountain climbers***

<u>Benefits</u> –
This activity helps in the development of the following skills:

- Enjoying the activity with friends

- Following the instructions of the game
- Understanding games with rules
- Body awareness
- Motor planning skills
- Observation & Imitation skills
- Reading, understanding & executing an action
- Use of multiple sensory processing skills
- Paying attention
- Counting the dots in a dice
- Cognitive skills- to understand "the number of times" as well as "the action to perform"

X
Team-Work Games

Team-Work Games

These games are very helpful for building a strong bond between friends. When kids learn to enjoy working together to complete a task/achieve a goal, it's the best way to build a bond, understand each other's skills & differences & learning to work together utilising their skills to the fullest.

Team-Work Games (For Younger kids)

Hold hands & walk together

Hold hands & walk together-

<u>Number of Participants</u> - 2 or more
<u>Equipment Required</u> – Any puzzles
<u>How to play</u> –

- Put some puzzles at one end & the board at the other end of the room.
- All children hold hands. Each picks up a puzzle.
- They all walk together holding hands & fix their puzzles turn wise.
- Then come back holding hands. Repeat till all the puzzles are completed.

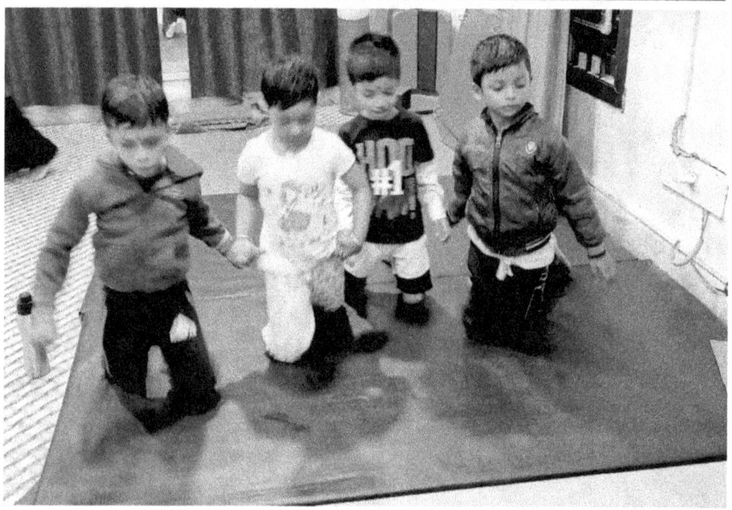

Hold hands & Kneel-walk together

Variation for older children –

- Older children can "hold hands & jump together." Or, "hold hands & kneel-walk together." To complete the activity.

<u>Benefits</u> –
This activity helps in the development of the following skills:

- Enjoying an activity with friends
- Developing bonding with friends
- Waiting for your friends to finish fixing puzzles & starting to walk together
- Impulse control
- Motor planning- while walking/kneel-walking/jumping together with friends holding hands, (not too fast that you move apart from the group, or too slow to be left behind)
- Team work

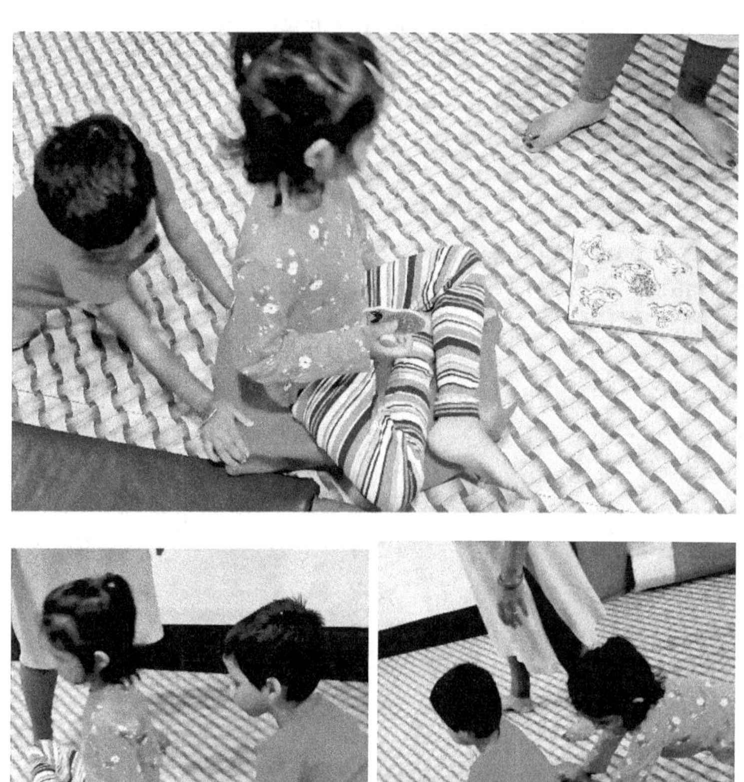

I Sit, You Push- Scooterboard

I Sit, You Push- Scooterboard

<u>Number of Participants</u> - 2 or more
<u>Equipment Required</u> –

- Scooterboard
- Puzzles

<u>How to play</u> –
Two kids can play this game, or make teams each with two players.

- You can use puzzles. Put equal number of puzzle pieces for each kid to complete. Keep the puzzles on one end & the puzzle boards on the other end of the room.
- For two kids, one child can sit on the scooterboard with a puzzle, while the other can push him/her in quadruped/bear position.
- He has to push his partner till the puzzle board. Then, push him back to the start to pick up another puzzle.
- Continue till all puzzles are completed taking turns to sit & push.

<u>Benefits-</u>
This activity helps in the development of the following skills:

- Team work
- Enjoying an activity with friends
- Proximal stability & strength while pushing the scooterboard
- Motor planning- To push the scooterboard with enough force that it moves but not so much that it knocks down the friend sitting on it
- Balancing your body on the scooterboard while your friend is pushing

Pass the Ball & throw into the bucket

Pass the Ball & throw into the bucket-

Number of Participants - 3 or more
Equipment Required –

- Small balls.
- Two buckets(one bucket has balls & the other is empty)

How to play –

- All the kids sit or stand in a line at a little distance from one another.
- One bucket (filled with balls) is placed at one end near the first kid.
- The other bucket(empty) is placed at the other end near the last child.
- The first kid picks up a ball from the bucket & passes to the next student who passes to the next. While passing the ball, they

should call the name of their friend & say "take the ball".

- The ball is passed from one student to the next in line until it reaches the last kid who throws it inside the bucket.
- You can give 3 chances to each kid & then change places.

<u>Benefits</u> -
This activity helps in the development of the following skills:

- Team work
- Bonding between friends
- Impulse control- to stand/sit at your place until the ball comes to you & to pass the ball sitting at a place
- Body awareness
- Bonding with friends
- Attention
- Waiting- for the ball to come to you & your turn to pass, or throw the ball
- Following rules of the game
- Observation & imitation skills

Carrying beads with spoon- Crossing Hurdles

Carrying beads with spoon-

This is a variation of the popular "Lemon race" we used to play in school.

<u>Number of Participants</u> - 4 or more

<u>Equipment Required</u> –

- Round beads/marbles,
- Spoons (1 for each kid),
- Small bottles to keep the beads

<u>How to play</u> –

- Make two-three teams, each with two kids.
- There are colourful beads(10 beads for each team) in one end & bottles(one for each team) at the other end of the room.
- Two kids of each team pick up a bead from the box of beads using their spoons, hold hands & walk together to the other end where they drop their beads inside their bottle.
- They must balance the beads using their spoons while walking together holding hands till their bottle.
- You can also give small hurdles to cross to make the activity more challenging.
- Whichever team completes their beads first wins.
- You can also play this game without the win/loose concept as a team work game.

Carrying beads with spoon- Kneel walking

Variation for older children –

- The students of each team can hold hands & kneel-walk together while balancing their beads in their spoons using their other hands & continue the game.

<u>Benefits</u> -
This activity helps in the development of the following skills:

- Following the instructions of the game
- Interaction with friends
- Team work
- Waiting - for your friend to pick up or put the bead inside the bottle & then walking together to get another bead
- Impulse control
- Fine motor skills
- Motor planning skills
- Balance & coordination
- Body awareness

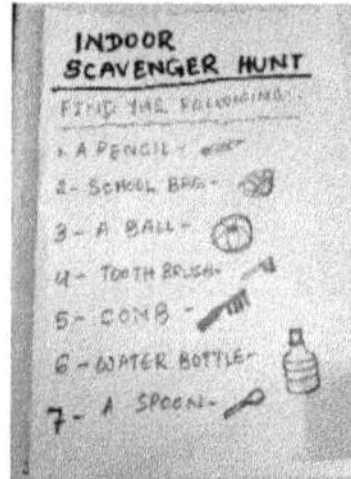

Scavenger Hunt

Scavenger Hunt-

This game can be modified for older & younger kids, the setting can be modified too. You can play Outside in the garden, or Inside school, or Inside house.

Number of Participants - 4 or more

Equipment Required –

- A list with names or pictures of some common items (can be different in different settings & for different age groups)
- A bag to collect your items

How to play –

- Make teams with at least two kids in each team.
- Each team is given a list of items they need to find & a bag to put their items.
- You can use your mobile timer to 3 minutes- 5 minutes.
- Whichever team can collect the maximum items within that time wins!
- You can also play it as a game without the concept of win/loose.

Example- For playing inside the house, you can add- (a spoon, a toy, a bottle, a scissor, a small ball, a pencil, etc)

For younger kids, you can add pictures along with the names of items.

For playing in a garden, you can add-(a green leaf, a yellow leaf, a blue flower, a feather, etc)

Benefits –

This activity helps in the development of the following skills:

- Team work
- Bonding between friends
- Enjoying an activity with friends
- Communication skills
- Following rules of the game
- Competitiveness

- Observation & imitation skills
- Problem solving skills

Team-Work Games (For Older kids)

Don't Spill me

Don't Spill me-

This is another interesting game kids enjoy playing.

Number of Participants - 4 or more

Equipment Required –

- Plastic cups/Paper cups (1 for each kid),

- Two small bowl/containers- one filled with water & one empty)

How to play –

- Make Two- three teams. Each team has at least two players.

- All children stand in a line, each holding a glass.
- There's a container of water at one end & an empty container at the other end.
- One kid fills his cup with water, then pours it into the next kid's glass.
- They keep on pouring water into the next kid's cup. The last kid pours water into the the empty container.
- You can set the timer to 2 minutes. When the timer goes off, whichever team has poured more water into their empty container wins.

Benefits –
This activity helps in the development of the following skills:

- Team work
- Bonding between friends
- Waiting- at your place for your friend to pass the water into your glass
- Coordination
- Following rules of the game
- Competitiveness
- Observation & imitation skills

Toss at the target

Toss at the target-

<u>Number of Participants</u> - 4 or more
    <u>Equipment Required</u> –

- Bucket of balls
- An empty bucket

<u>How to play</u> –

- Make Two- three teams. Each team has two players.
- Two kids stand at some distance facing each other.
- One kid holds a bucket. The other kid throws small balls one by one at his partner who tries to catch them in his bucket.
- You can give total 10 or 20 balls to each team.
- The team which has caught the most number of balls in their bucket, wins.

You can also play it as a game without the concept of win/loose.
<u>Benefits</u> –
This activity helps in the development of the following skills:

- Team work
- Bonding between friends
- Impulse control- to stand at your place holding the bucket when your friend throws the ball
- Motor planning skills required to throw the ball inside the bucket standing at a small distance & also to catch a ball using the bucket
- Body awareness to hold the bucket with both hands & catch the ball using the bucket
- Bonding with friends
- Competitiveness
- Attention
- Following rules of the game
- Observation & imitation skills

Fish bowl Game

Fish bowl Game-

Number of Participants - 4 or more
Equipment Required –

- A fish bowl/any container
- Chits of paper

How to play –

- Make Two- three teams. Each team has atleast two players.
- Write down the names of some common objects in the chits.
- For primary school & even secondary school students, you can also write the names of *persons* (Community helpers/Famous personalities or even Family members if playing with family), *places or any other category names* for this game.

- One player of each team picks up a chit, & describes the word without telling the word.
- The other player has to guess the word within one minute.
- One point for each correct guess.
- The team who makes maximum correct guesses, wins.

You can also play it as a game without the concept of win/loose.
Example- If the word in the chit is **"Mango"**, you can say- "This is a yellow juicy fruit which has one seed. We get it in summers."
Benefits –
This game helps in developing the following skills:

- Enjoying an activity with friends
- Communication skills
- Interacting with friends
- Vocabulary
- Imagination skills
- Attention
- Cognitive skills
- Listening skills
- Competitiveness

Charades

Charades-

This is another interesting game we all enjoy playing.
Number of Participants - 4 or more
Equipment Required –

- A bowl/any container
- Chits of paper

How to play –

- Make Two- three teams. Each team has atleast two players.
- Write down the names of some common objects, or, action words in the chits.
- For primary school & even secondary school students, you can also write the names of *persons* (Community helpers/Famous personalities or even Family members if playing with family), *or movie names.*
- This is quite similar to the fish bowl game except for, one player of each team picks up a chit, & acts out the word without <u>telling the word or saying anything</u>.
- The other player has to guess the word within one minute.
- One point for each correct guess.
- The team who makes maximum correct guesses, wins.
- For younger kids, you can skip the points part.

<u>*Example*</u>- If the word in the chit is **_"Doctor"_**, you can act out wearing a stethoscope & giving injection, or checking for pulse rate.

<u>Benefits</u> –

This game helps in developing the following skills:

- Enjoying an activity with friends
- Communication skills
- Vocabulary
- Following rules of the game
- Interacting with friends
- Imagination skills
- Cognitive skills
- Social etiquettes
- Problem solving skills
- Learning different life roles
- Self confidence
- Learning independence in everyday skills

XI

Games with Beads, Coins & Pegs

Games with Beads, Coins & Pegs

Pass the bead with spoon

Pass the bead with spoon-

<u>Number of Participants</u> - 3 or more
<u>Equipment Required</u> –

- Round beads/marbles,
- Spoons (1 for each kid),
- A small bowl/bottle to keep the beads

<u>How to play</u> –

- All children sit in a line, each holding a spoon.
- There's a box of colourful beads at one end & an empty bowl or bottle at the other end.
- One kid picks up a bead from the box of beads using his spoon, then drops that bead to the next kid's spoon.
- They keep on passing the beads using their spoons. The last kid drops the bead into the bottle.
- Take turns to change positions after passing 3 beads.

<u>Benefits</u> -
This activity helps in the development of the following skills:

- Following the instructions of the game
- Simple communication skills
- Waiting for your turn
- Impulse control
- Team work
- Identification of colours
- Sequencing skills
- Paying attention when it's your turn
- Fine motor skills

- Motor planning required to pass the bead to another child's spoon or to a bottle without droping it

Where is the bead?

Where is the bead?-

Number of Participants - 3 or more
    Equipment Required –

- Small beads, or coins, or even letter/number puzzles can be used

- Three or four Stacking cups or small bowls can be used

How to play –

- All children sit forming a circle.
- The teacher places three or four small bowls at the center.
- Now, the teacher hides a small bead/coin under one of the cups showing everyone.
- Then, the teacher shuffles the cups a few times. The students must pay attention to see where the bead is being moved.
- The teacher asks a student, "where's the bead?" If he answers correctly, he gets a point or a high-five.
- If the student is wrong, the teacher can ask another student or just show where the bead is.
- The game continues for a few rounds. Make sure each student gets the chance to answer.

Benefits -

This activity helps in the development of the following skills:

- Following the instructions of the game
- Attention Span
- Paying attention when it's your turn to answer
- Impulse control
- Memory
- Confidence

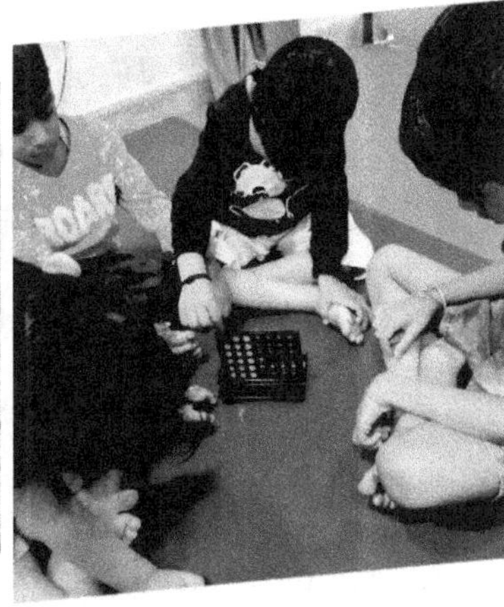

Count & Put Coins

Count & Put Coins-

<u>Number of Participants</u> - 2 or more
<u>Equipment Required</u> –

- Connect 4 game & its coins

<u>How to play</u> –

- All children sit in a circle.
- The students can each put a coin inside the slots of the Connect 4 turnwise.
- To make it challenging, teacher can say a number to each student turnwise. They can count & put that number of coins in the slots.
- Game continues till all the slots of the Connect 4 are full.

Example- Teacher can say- "Aman put 3 red coins." "Khush put 4 yellow coins". "Sibya put 5 red coins".
<u>Variation</u> –

- You can exclude the counting part & instead simply assign a row to each student to put the coins turnwise.

Example- Aman will put a coin in the first row, next, Khush will put in the second row, Sibya will put in the third row, again Aman will put another coin in the first row,etc.
<u>Benefits-</u>
This activity helps in the development of the following skills:

- Enjoying an activity with friends
- Following the instructions of the game
- Waiting for your turn
- Counting skills
- Paying attention when it's your turn to put the coins & the number of coins
- Listening skills

- Sequencing skills
- Fine motor skills
- Visual perception

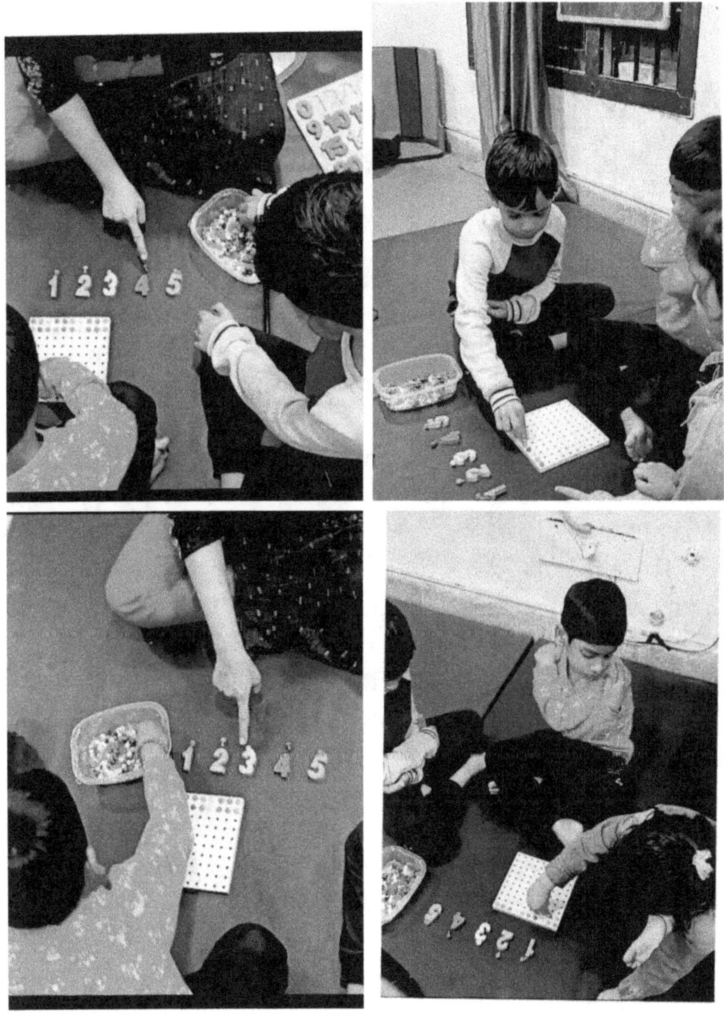

Fixing pegs correspondent to the number

Fixing pegs correspondent to the number-

<u>Number of Participants</u> - 2 or more
    <u>Equipment Required</u> –

- Colour Pegs & a pegboard, or, Colour beads & a thread.
- Number puzzles.

<u>How to play</u> –

- All children sit in a circle.
- Teacher puts numbers 1-10 in a row & 10 different colour pegs, one colour peg next to each number.
- You can use numbers 1-5 & 5 different colour pegs for younger kids.
- Next, teacher calls out a number, & the first student fixes the colur peg next to that number.(He has to take the peg from the box of colour pegs).
- All students take turns to fix the colour pegs according to the number called out by the teacher.

<u>Example</u>- 1-Pink, 2- Red, 3-Yellow, 4-Green, 5-Blue. When teacher says "Khush fix 1", Khush fixes Pink peg. Teacher says "Krrish fix 2", Krrish fixes Red peg & so on.
    <u>Variation</u>-

- Instead of colour pegs, colour beads can be used. One colour bead for each number, 1-10.
- Each student can thread the colour bead correspondent to the number called out, then pass to the next student.
- Repeat for a few rounds.

<u>Benefits</u>-

This activity helps in the development of the following skills:

- Identification of numbers
- Waiting for your turn
- Cognitive skills to understand the rules of the game
- Attention
- Listening skills
- Confidence
- Fine motor skills
- Visual perception
- Observation skills

XII
Copying Games

Copying Games

These games focus mainly upon the skills required for activities in school like-

- Working together,
- Developing the discipline,
- Obervation & imitation skills,
- Visual perception skills which are very essential for reading, writing & other daily tasks
- Imagination & Creativity
- Confidence

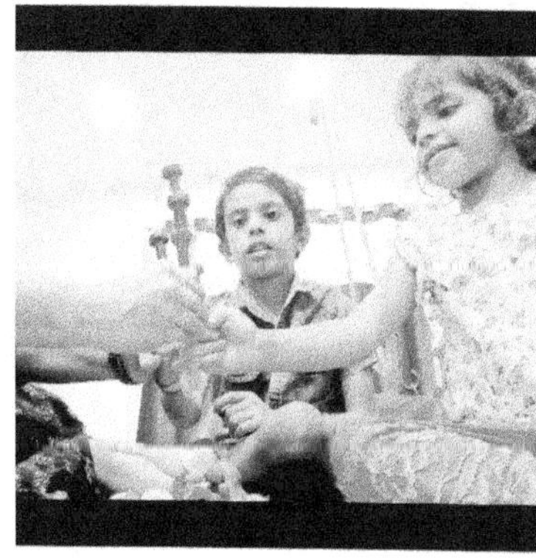 

Copy the sequence

**Copy the sequence-**

<u>Number of Participants</u> - 2 or more

 <u>Equipment Required</u> –

- Colour Pegs or colour blocks that can be fixed one on the other.

<u>How to play</u> –

- All children sit in a circle.
- Teacher starts by fixing the colour pegs in a sequence. You can use 4 or 5 pegs to make a pattern.
- All students make the same pattern using the colour pegs.

<u>*Example-*</u> *Blue Yellow Red Green*

<u>Variation</u> -

- To make the game more challenging, the teacher can name 4 or 5 colours in a sequence.
- All the students have to listen, remember & make that pattern with the colour pegs.

<u>Benefits-</u>

This activity helps in the development of the following skills:

- Enjoying an activity with friends
- Observation & imitation skills
- Waiting for your friends to complete their designs
- Cognitive skills to understand the rules of the game
- Attention
- Sequencing skills
- Listening skills
- Confidence
- Fine motor skills
- Visual perception

Copy the design - with Connect 4 coins

Copy the design -

<u>Number of Participants</u> - 2 or more
<u>Equipment Required</u> –

- Colour beads or Connect 4 coins

<u>How to play</u> –

- All children sit in a circle.
- Teacher shows an example by forming a letter using the beads or coins.
- Next, all students have to make the letter using beads or coins.
- Teacher can also ask them to make simple shapes of Triangle/ square/circle using beads.

 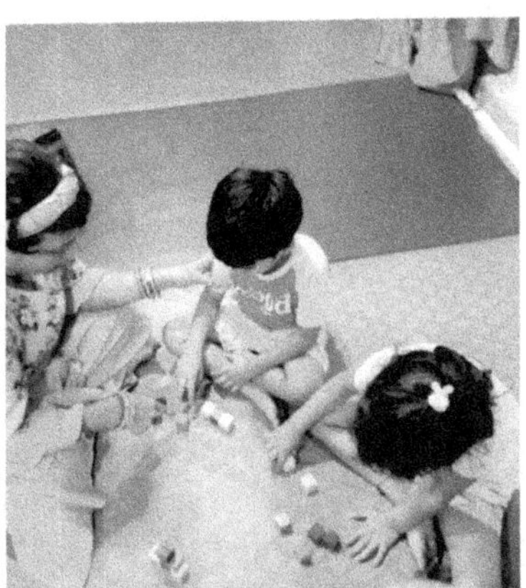

Copy the design- with colour blocks

<u>Variation-</u>

- You can use colour blocks to make a 3-D design.

- All students have to copy the same design.

<u>Benefits-</u>
This activity helps in the development of the following skills:

- Enjoying an activity with friends
- Observation & imitation skills
- Waiting for your friends to complete their designs
- Cognitive skills to understand the rules of the game
- Attention
- Motor planning
- Confidence
- Fine motor skills
- Visual perception skills

Copy the design with playdough

<u>Copy the design with playdough-</u>

<u>Number of Participants</u> - 2 or more
  <u>Equipment Required</u> –

- Colour Playdough

<u>How to play</u> –

- All children sit in a circle.
- Teacher shows an example by forming a letter or a shape using playdough
- Next, all students have to make the letter using playdough
- Teacher can also make some simple objects/animals using playdough & the students can copy.

<u>Benefits-</u>
This activity helps in the development of the following skills:

- Enjoying an activity with friends
- Observation & imitation skills
- Design copying
- Attention
- Appreciating your own work & the work of your friends
- Imagination & creativity
- Listening skills
- Confidence
- Fine motor skills
- Visual perception

Paper Folding

Paper Folding-

Number of Participants - 2 or more
   Equipment Required –

- Colour Papers

How to play –

- All children sit in a circle.
- Teacher starts by folding a piece of paper making some simple objects like a "Paper boat", or a "Rocket".
- Next, all students have to copy the teacher step by step to make the object.
- Teacher can start by teaching simple folding of paper into one half or two halves then proceed to making objects/crafts.
- You can include cutting with safety scissors & pasting activities if the children have developed scissor cutting skills.

Benefits-
This activity helps in the development of the following skills:

- Enjoying an activity with friends
- Appreciationg your own work & the work of your friends
- Team work
- Observation & imitation skills
- Imagination & Creativity
- Cognitive skills to understand the rules of the game
- Attention
- Sequencing skills
- Listening skills
- Confidence
- Fine motor skills

- Visual perception

XIII
Auditory Processing/ Listening Games

Auditory Processing/Listening Games

These games focus mainly upon the skills required for activities in school like-

- Developing the discipline,
- Obervation & imitation skills,
- Socialization skills
- Auditory perception skills which are very essential for understanding instructions, speech & language, responding to name,etc.
- Cognitive skills
- Confidence

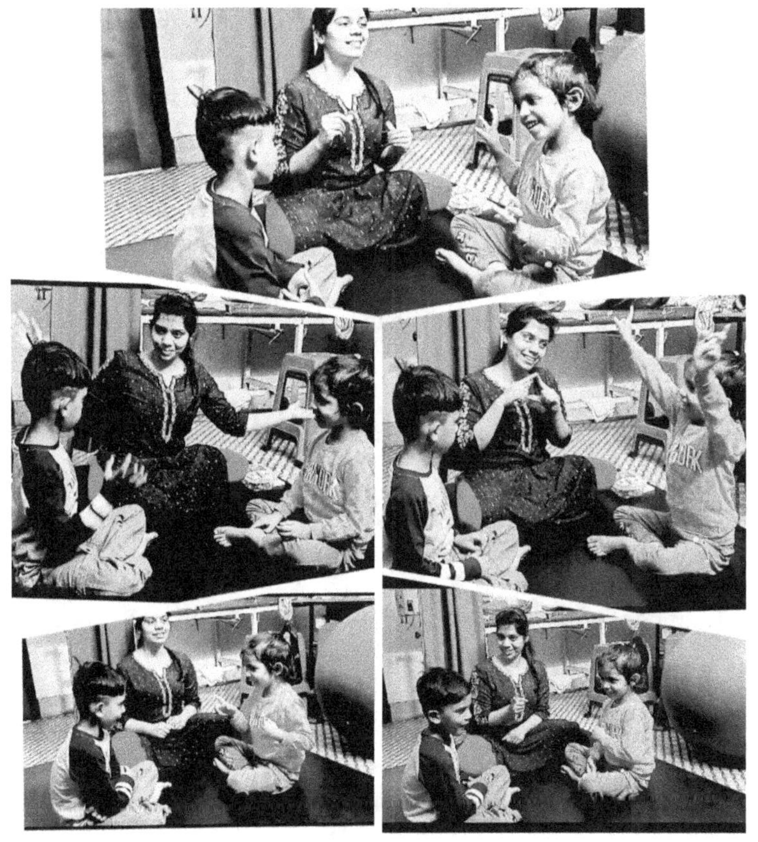

Complete the Rhymes

Complete the Rhymes-

Number of Participants - 3 or more
Equipment Required – None
How to play –

- All the kids sit in a line.

- The teacher starts by singing the first line of a popular rhymes. The first student then sings the next line of the rhyme. Each child continues with the next line of the rhyme until it's completed.
- Each student must sing their line & wait for the next participant to sing the next line.

<u>Benefits</u> –
This activity helps in the development of the following skills:

- Enjoying an activity with friends
- Team work
- Listening skills
- Communication skills
- Vocabulary
- Observation & imitation skills
- Cognitive skills to understand the rules of the game
- Attention
- Confidence

Let's Whisper

Let's Whisper-

<u>Number of Participants</u> - 3 or more
<u>Equipment Required</u> – None
<u>How to play</u> –

- All the kids sit/stand in a line at a small distance from one another.
- The teacher has a chit in which a sentence is written. She starts by whispering that line in the ears of the student standing at the front.
- The first student whispers the line to the next student who whispers to the next. Each kid continues whispering to the next kid.
- Finally, the last student loudly tells the sentence.
- The teacher shows the paper to show if it's correct or wrong.

<u>Benefits</u> –
This activity helps in the development of the following skills:

- Enjoying an activity with friends
- Team work
- Listening skills
- Communication skills
- Vocabulary
- Observation & imitation skills
- Cognitive skills to understand the rules of the game
- Attention
- Confidence

Answer the Questions

Answer the Questions-

Number of Participants - 2 or more
   Equipment Required – None
   How to play –

- All the kids sit in a line.
- The teacher reads out a short story. Story can be as short as one-two paragraphs.
- Then, the teacher asks questions from the story turnwise to each student.
- When a student answers correctly, everyone claps for him/her.

Benefits –
This activity helps in the development of the following skills:

- Listening skills
- Communication skills
- Vocabulary
- Waiting for your name to be called
- Observation skills
- Cognitive skills
- Attention
- Confidence to answer questions infront of others
- Encouraging friends
- Competitiveness

Story time Clap

Story time Clap-

Number of Participants - 3 or more
  Equipment Required – None
  How to play –

- The teacher reads out a short story or a paragraph. Whenever a particular word comes, all students have to clap. The word chosen should be used multiple times in the story the teacher is reading.

*Example-*I have a small white Cat in my house. My cat loves to drink milk. My cat loves to play with me. My cat can climb on trees. I love my cat very much.
  Everyone has to clap every time they hear the word, "Cat".
  Variation-

- You can make it more challenging by adding two words in which they have to do some action.

*Example-*Clap with the word, "Cat" & Tap on desk with the word "Dog".
  Benefits –
  This activity helps in the development of the following skills:

- Listening skills
- Auditory perception skills to clap only when you hear the word "Cat"
- Observation skills
- Cognitive skills to understand the rules of the game
- Attention
- Confidence

XIV
Music Games

Music Games

These are fun & interesting rule based games that have numerous benefits. These games encourage learning while having fun.

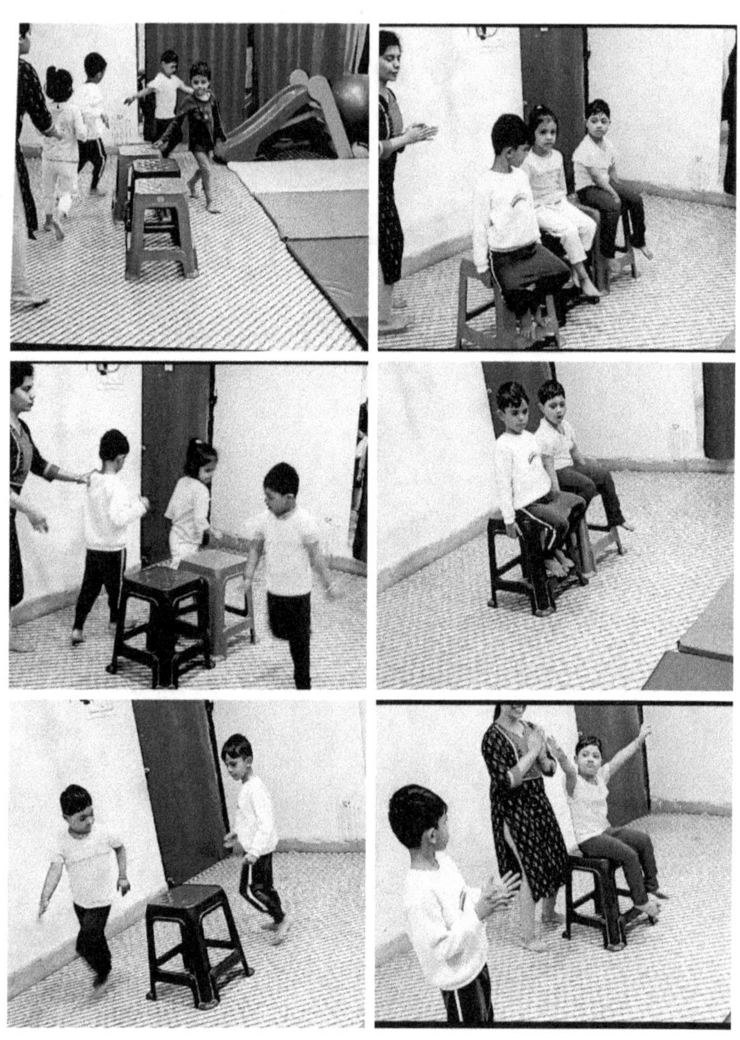

Music Chair

Music Chair-

This is another interesting game we all enjoy playing.

Number of Participants - 3 or more

Equipment Required –

- Chairs (Number of chairs=number of participants)
- Music

How to play –

- Put the chairs at a little distance from each other in a line.
- You can put the chairs in any other arrangement also. The chairs can face one side, or one facing front & the next facing back.
- You can also place all chairs at the center if there are less number of participants.
- When music is played, all kids move around the chairs.
- When music stops, they need to immediately sit on a chair.
- Remove one chair in each round. Start music again.
- Whichever participant couldn't find a chair to sit is eliminated.
- The last kid who sits on a chair when music stops, wins the game.

Benefits –

This activity helps in the development of the following skills:

- Enjoying an activity with friends
- Listening skills
- Observation & imitation skills
- Cognitive skills to understand the rules of the game
- Impulse control
- Attention
- Confidence

Music Chair with Actions

Music Chair with Actions-

This is similar to music Chair with a little variation.

<u>Number of Participants</u> - 3 or more

<u>Equipment Required</u> –

- Chairs (Number of chairs=number of participants)
- Music

<u>How to play</u> –

- Put the chairs close to each other each other forming a circle.
- You can put the chairs in any other arrangement also. The chairs can face one side, or one facing front & the next facing back.
- When music is played, all kids move around the chairs.
- When music stops, each student needs to maintain a position until the music starts again.
- They can maintain quadruped, or bear or kneeling or squatting, any position. Each participant must quickly make a static position when music stops & start moving when music starts.

<u>Variation</u>-

- You can add – If someone moves when music is topped, he/she is eliminated. Or, if someone can't think of any position when music stops, they are eliminated.
- The last student who is not eliminated, wins.
- You can also paste pictures of different postures on each chair. Whichever student stops near a chair, has to maintain that position as shown in picture.

Example-One leg standing, Plank, Bear position, Kneeling position, etc.

<u>Benefits</u> –

This activity helps in the development of the following skills:

- Enjoying an activity with friends

- Team work
- Listening skills
- Impulse control
- Observation & imitation skills
- Cognitive skills to understand the rules of the game
- Motor planning skills
- Postural control
- Attention
- Confidence

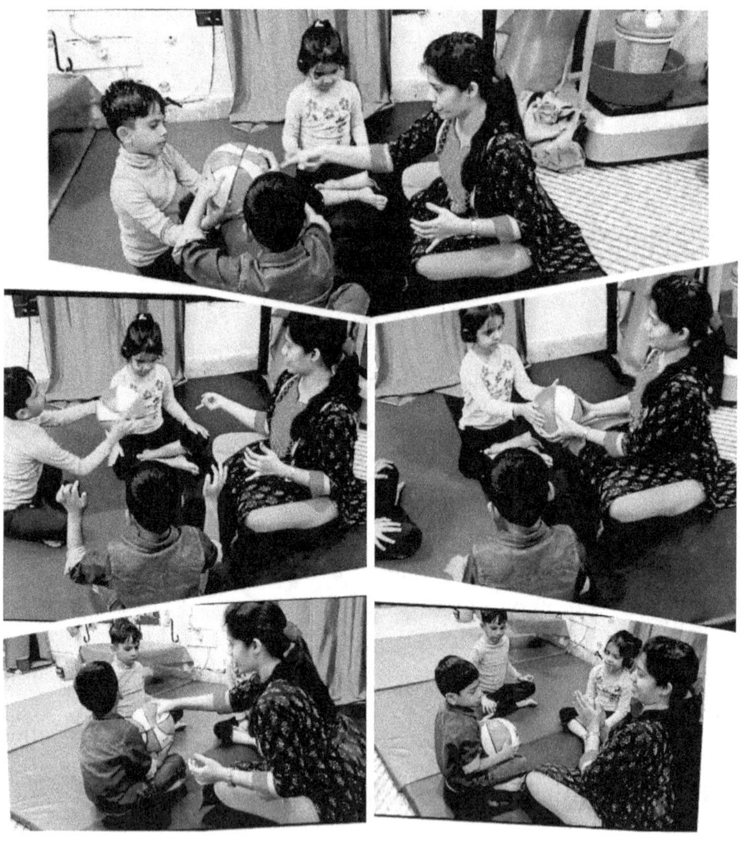

<u>Pass the ball till music stops</u>

<u>Pass the ball till music stops-</u>

<u>Number of Participants</u> - 3 or more
<u>Equipment Required</u> –

- Music
- A ball

<u>How to play</u> –

- All participants sit in a circle.
- When music starts, they need to pass the ball to the next player quickly.
- When music stops, the kid who has the ball has to do a short task the teacher says.
- Task can be anything- Sing a rhyme, Tell a short story, Answer a question, etc.
- When his task is over, play the music again & start passing the ball.

<u>Variation for younger kids</u> –

- You can play this game with younger kids & pre-schoolers also.
- Whenever music stops, ask everyone, "who has the ball?" "who has the ball?", they can answer the name of the kid- "Aman has the ball".
- You can give an easy task like – whoever has the ball, can fix a puzzle, or thread a bead.

<u>Benefits</u> –
This activity helps in the development of the following skills:

- Enjoying an activity with friends
- Getting to know your friends
- Listening skills
- Communication skills
- Observation & imitation skills
- Cognitive skills to understand the rules of the game
- Attention
- Confidence

Jump with music

Jump with music-

<u>Number of Participants</u> - 2 or more
    <u>Equipment Required</u> –

- Music
- Hoola-hoops
- Alphabet puzzles

<u>How to play</u> –

- Place 5-6 hoola-hoops on the floor making a large circle.
- Inside each hoola -hoop place an alphabet.
- When music starts, the participants start jumping from one hoola-hoop to the other in clockwise direction.
- They need to coordinate their jumps in such a manner that no two players can enter one hoola-hoop at a time
- When the music stops, each participant has to name the letter inside the hoola-hoop they are standing & 2-3 words starting with that letter.
- Then, music starts again & the game continues. You cannot repeat a word which you or any other participant has told before.

<u>Benefits</u> –
This activity helps in the development of the following skills:

- Enjoying an activity with friends
- Team work
- Listening skills
- Vocabulary
- Observation & imitation skills
- Cognitive skills to understand the rules of the game
- Attention

- Confidence
- Motor planning

XV

Tactile Perception & Body awareness games

Tactile Perception & Body awareness games

Find by Touch

Find by Touch-

<u>Number of Participants</u> - 2 or more
  <u>Equipment Required</u> –

- A list with names or pictures of some common items (can be different in different settings & for different age groups)
- Bags to keep your items (one for each child)
- Some common small objects
- Puzzles can also be used

<u>How to play</u> –

- All students sit in a line with their bags.
- There is a list of items on a paper.
- Each child is given some items from the list inside their bags.
- The teacher can describe the first object on the list. Or, the object can be held up for everyone to see.
- All the students then close their eyes & use their hands <u>without looking</u>to find the designated objects by *"touch & feel only"*. Whoever has the item, raises his hand & says- "I have it".
- The game continues until all the items on that list are found.
- The students are encouraged to manipulate the objects & feel for the corners, roundness, texture, & size.
- Have the students be the leader & try to describe what to look for.

To hide in the bags Items can be – a ping pong ball, a spoon, a small toy car, a pencil, a smiley ball, an eraser, a key, a fruit, a flower, a hanky, etc)

For younger kids, you can add pictures along with the names of items or, large shape/letter/number puzzles can be used.

<u>Benefits</u> –
This activity helps in the development of the following skills:

- Team work
- Following the instructions of the game
- Perception of touch
- Waiting for your turn
- Impulse control
- Cognitive skills
- Fine motor skills

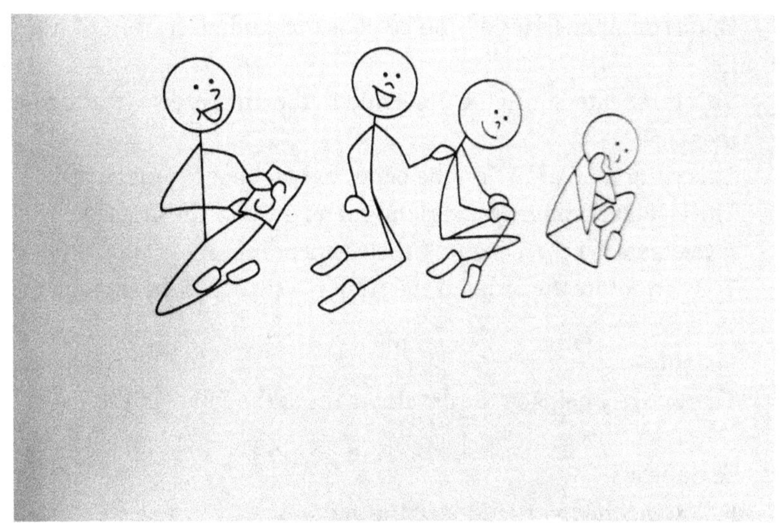

Pass it on

Pass it on-

<u>Number of Participants</u> - 2 or more
   <u>Equipment Required</u> –

- Pencil
- Paper

<u>How to play</u> –

- Make 2-3 teams with atleast two players in each team.
- The students of each team sit in train-style, facing one another's back.
- The last student in the line is given a chit of paper in which a letter/shape/number is written. He draws the same letter, number, or shape on the person's back who's sitting directly infront of him *with his fingers*. That student then draws the same shape/number/letter on the back of the student infront of him/her.
- This is repeated until the first child in the line receives the tactile message.
- This child then draws on the paper or blackboard what was felt.
- The last child in line verifies the correctness of the message.
- If they make a correct guess, they get a point.
- You can rotate the order of the students sitting in the line.

<u>Benefits</u> –
This activity helps in the development of the following skills:

- Team work
- Following the instructions of the game
- Perception of touch
- Waiting for your turn
- Impulse control
- Cognitive skills
- Fine motor skills

Dress up Relay

Dress up Relay-

This is a popular game played in schools
Number of Participants - 2 or more
Equipment Required –

- Clothing: Large shirts, Coats, Sweaters, Pants, Socks, Shoes, Mittens, Hats

How to play –

- Draw two parallel lines 10-12 feet apart using chalk or masking tape marking as the "start" & the "finish" lines.
- All children line up on the "start" line. The teacher puts an item of clothing on the "finish" line, directly across from each child.

- The children are asked to "Kneel-walk", "Hop", "Bearwalk", "Skip", or "Run" to their piece of clothing & put it on.
- After dressing, each child moves in the designated manner to the "start" line.

<u>Benefits</u> –
This activity helps in the development of the following skills:

- Following the instructions of the game
- Perception of touch
- Body awareness
- Motor planning required to dress up
- Impulse control
- Cognitive skills
- Fine motor skills
- Competitiveness

Turtle Race

Turtle Race-

<u>Number of Participants</u> - 2 or more
  <u>Equipment Required</u> –

- Turtle shells- Small beanbags, jackets, pillow, puzzle pieces, etc.
- Start & finish lines, 12-15 feet apart- masking tape or chalk or yarn may be used

<u>How to play</u> –

- Draw two parallel lines 12-15 feet apart using chalk or masking tape marking as the "start" & the "finish" lines.
- All children line up on the "start" line. The teacher puts items like pillows, or jackets or beanbags or puzzle piece on the child's back as "shell".
- The children are asked to crawl to the finish line trying not to loose their shell.
- The student who can reach the finish line with most of their "shell" intact, wins!

<u>Variation-</u>

- The students can do "Crabwalk" instead of crawl & balance the objects on their stomachs.
- You can also do this activity without the concept of win/loose

<u>Benefits</u> –
This activity helps in the development of the following skills:

- Following the instructions of the game
- Perception of touch
- Body awareness
- Motor planning required to keep holding the object on your back/stomach while doing the animal walk
- Observation & Imitation skills
- Impulse control

- Cognitive skills
- Competitiveness

Animal Walks

Animal Walks -

Number of Participants - 3 or more
  Equipment Required –

- Chits of paper
- A bowl/basket

How to play –

- Write down a bunch of animal names on the chits of papers & put them in the basket.

- Whosever name is called, picks up a chit, reads the name of the animal on the paper & has to walk like the chosen animal across the classroom.
- The other students have to guess which "animal walk" he is doing.
- You can also make a mark, like the students have to make the correct guess before the student reaches the door, to make it more fun.

Variation-

- You can pick up a chit. Whichever animal is written,
- The kids can do animal walks from one end to the other end on a playground.
- They can be given a starting & a finishing line

Benefits –
This activity helps in the development of the following skills:

- Following the instructions of the game
- Body awareness
- Motor planning required to perform the required animal walk & to not bump against their friends while doing the animal walk
- Observation & Imitation skills
- Impulse control
- Cognitive skills

Hand & Feet Mat

Hand & Feet Mat-

<u>Number of Participants</u> - 3 or more
    <u>Equipment Required</u> –

- Pattern mat with hands & feet drawn on it. Or, you can draw simple patterns on the floor using chalk/marker.
- Give some puzles to complete. It's similar to hopscotch game.
- All students stand in a line. The teacher can first show them how to jump in a pattern over the mat/ chalk patterns.
- Each participant picks a puzzle & starts jumping in the same pattern as shown by the teacher, & fixes his puzzle.
- Take turns to jump till all the puzzles are completed.

<u>Benefits</u> –
This activity helps in the development of the following skills:

- Following the instructions of the game
- Waiting for your turn
- Observation & Imitation skills
- Body awareness
- Motor planning required to perform the activity
- Impulse control
- Cognitive skills

One-leg standing holding hands

One-leg standing holding hands-

Number of Participants - 3 or more
   Equipment Required –

· None

How to play –

· The students stand closely holding hands in a circle or in a line.
· Teacher commands- "Right leg up". Everyone lifts their right leg & try to stand in one leg holding hands of their friend.
· Teacher can count 1-10 & then change command- "Left leg up".
· The students need to balance with one leg while holding each other's hands.

<u>Benefits</u> –

This activity helps in the development of the following skills:

- Team work
- Observation & Imitation skills
- Body awareness
- Motor planning required to perform the activity
- Balance & Coordination
- Listening skills
- Impulse control
- Cognitive skills

Roll Roll & Pass- Stacking rings

Roll Roll & Pass-

<u>Number of Participants</u> - 4 or more
   <u>Equipment Required</u> –

- Small balls
- Small buckets/Small tubs
- Stacking rings can also be used instead of balls

<u>How to play</u> –

- Make two-three teams, each team with two players.
- Place small balls in a tub at one end of the room(equal numbers for each team) & the empty tub at the other end of the room (one for each team).
- You can use a small rope at the middle as the demarcation " Place for passing the ball".
- If there are two players, take turns for each player to pass the ball & to put inside the empty tub. If there are teams, each has two players.
- One player of each team picks up a ball placed at one end, rolls to the rope, where his partner is, gives the ball to his partner, who then rolls to the other end & puts the ball inside the empty tub placed at the other end of the room. While the other kid rolls back to pick up another ball.
- Game continues till all the balls are completed.
- The team who completes their balls first, wins.
- You can also use stacking rings instead of balls for this game. Put the rings at one end & its stand at the other end. Game continues the same as above untill all the rings are completed.

You can also play it as a game without the concept of win/loose.
<u>Benefits-</u>
This activity helps in the development of the following skills:

- Bonding with friends
- Team work

- Body awareness
- Motor planning required to perform the activity
- Problem solving skills
- Cognitive skills

XVI
Jumping Games

Jumping Games

Jump on Patterns

Jump on Patterns-

<u>Number of Participants</u> - 2 or more
  <u>Equipment Required</u> –

- Hoola-hoops
- Any puzzles

<u>How to play</u> –

- Place 5-10 hoola-hoops on the floor making patterns in which to jump.
- Give some puzles to complete. It's similar to hopscotch game.
- All students stand in a line. The teacher can first show them how to jump in a pattern over the hoola-hoops.
- Each participant picks a puzzle & starts jumping in the same pattern as shown by the teacher, & fixes his puzzle.
- Take turns to jump till all the puzzles are completed.
- You can give a pattern simple or challenging depending on the age & level of the participants. *You can use two legs in one circle/ one leg in one circle/ one-leg hopping/turn & jump/jumping sidewise,etc.*

<u>Benefits-</u>
This activity helps in the development of the following skills:

- Following the instructions of the game
- Body awareness
- Motor planning required to perform the activity (jumping on different patterns)
- Observation & Imitation skills
- Waiting for your turn
- Cognitive skills

Jump on Shape

Jump on Shape-

<u>Number of Participants</u> - 3 or more
   <u>Equipment Required</u> –

- Hoola-hoops
- Shape puzzles/ Large shapes cut on pattern paper

<u>How to play</u> –

- Place 5-10 hoola-hoops on the floor making patterns in which to jump.
- Place different shape puzzles inside each hoola hoop from start till end where the puzzle board is placed.
- Alternatively, you can paste large shapes cut from pattern paper pasted on the floor in patterns.
- When you start jumping, jump over all the hoola hoops with similar shapes. Designate a different shape to each child to jump over.
- All students stand in a line. The teacher can first show them how to jump over the shapes & reach the puzzle board.
- Each kid can jump inside a hoola hoop, pick his designated shape, jump to the next hoola hoop (where another similar shape is placed), keep jumping & collecting his shapes until he/she reaches the puzzle board where he fixes them all.

Example-Som will collect all the squares, Kakul will collect all the circles & Sibhi will collect all the triangles.

- Take turns to jump till all the puzzles are completed.
- You can give a pattern simple or challenging depending on the age & level of the participants.

<u>Benefits-</u>
This activity helps in the development of the following skills:

- Following the instructions of the game

- Body awareness
- Motor planning required to perform the activity
- Impulse control
- Observation & Imitation skills
- Waiting for your turn
- Cognitive skills to follow the rules (to jump & pick up the particular shape assigned to you)

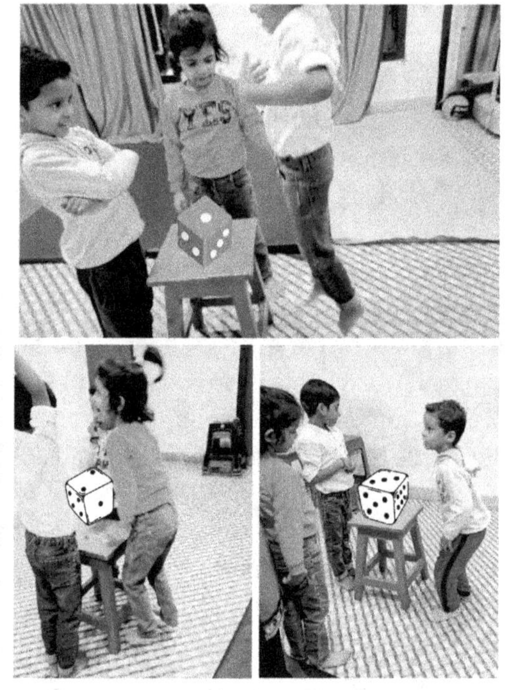

Jump with Dice

Jump with Dice-

Number of Participants - 3 or more

Equipment Required –

- Ludo Dice

How to play –

- All participants stand around a stool/table.
- The first kid starts by rolling the dice on the stool.
- Whichever number comes, he has to jump that many times & then pass the dice to the next kid.
- That kid rolls his dice again, counts the dots & jumps according to the number on the dice.
- Continue the game for a few rounds.

Benefits -
This activity helps in the development of the following skills:

- Following the instructions of the game
- Body awareness
- Motor planning required to perform the activity
- Counting
- Thinking processing skills
- Observation & Imitation skills
- Waiting for your turn
- Cognitive skills

I Jump, You count

I Jump, You count-

<u>Number of Participants</u> - 2 or more
<u>Equipment Required</u> –

- Trampoline

<u>How to play</u> –

- For two kids, one child can jump on the trampoline while the other can count standing on the floor.
- For more than two kids, take turns so that two or three can jump on the trampoline holding hands while one counts standing on

the floor.
- You can ask to count 1-20 or 20-1 or randomly any other sequence like- 20-50, A-Z, etc.
- Take turns to jump & count.

Benefits-
This activity helps in the development of the following skills:

- Following the instructions of the game
- Body awareness
- Motor planning required to perform the activity
- Counting
- Team work
- Thinking processing skills
- Observation & Imitation skills
- Waiting for your turn
- Cognitive skills

Jump over Rolling bottle

Jump over Rolling bottle-

<u>Number of Participants</u> - 3 or more
<u>Equipment Required</u> –

- Bottle or anything cylindrical that rolls.

<u>How to play</u> –

- All participants stand in a line one behind the other close to each other.
- The teacher stands in the front & rolls the bottle towards the kids.
- The first kid jumps quickly over the bottle & comes front. Then the next kid jumps over the bottle & moves forward.
- The teacher should roll the bottle with a speed that it reaches till the last kid jumps over the bottle.
- Continue rolling from the other side now.

<u>Benefits-</u>
This activity helps in the development of the following skills:

- Following the instructions of the game
- Enjoying an activity with friends
- Body awareness
- Motor planning required to perform the activity
- Team work
- Thinking processing skills
- Observation & Imitation skills
- Performing the task when your turn comes- understanding your turn
- Cognitive skills
- Confidence

XVII
Hoola-hoop Games

Hoola-hoop Games

Hoop Walk

Hoop Walk -

<u>Number of Participants</u> - 2 or more
    <u>Equipment Required</u> –

- Hoola hoops (one for each group)
- Ropes of the same length (one for each group)

<u>How to play</u> –

- Draw two parallel lines using chalk or masking tape marking as the "start" & the "finish" lines.
- You can make two or three groups each with two students
- All children line up on the "start" line. Each group has a hoola hoop & a rope.
- One student of each group stands inside a hoola hoop at the "start" line. Ropes are tied to all the hoola hoops.
- The other student of each group holds the rope & stands at the "Finish" line. When teacher commands "start", the students holding the ropes pull the ropes*(tied to hoola hoops)* torwards themselves with their partners walking inside the hoola hoop as it moves.
- The group that reaches the finish line first wins.
- As a Variation, you can give some puzzles to complete turnwise for each group.

<u>Benefits</u> –
This activity helps in the development of the following skills:

- Following the instructions of the game
- Body awareness
- Motor planning required to perform the activity (pulling the hoola hoop & moving at the same time, walking inside the hoola

hoop & not moving out of it)
- Simple communication
- Bonding with friends
- Team work
- Cooperation

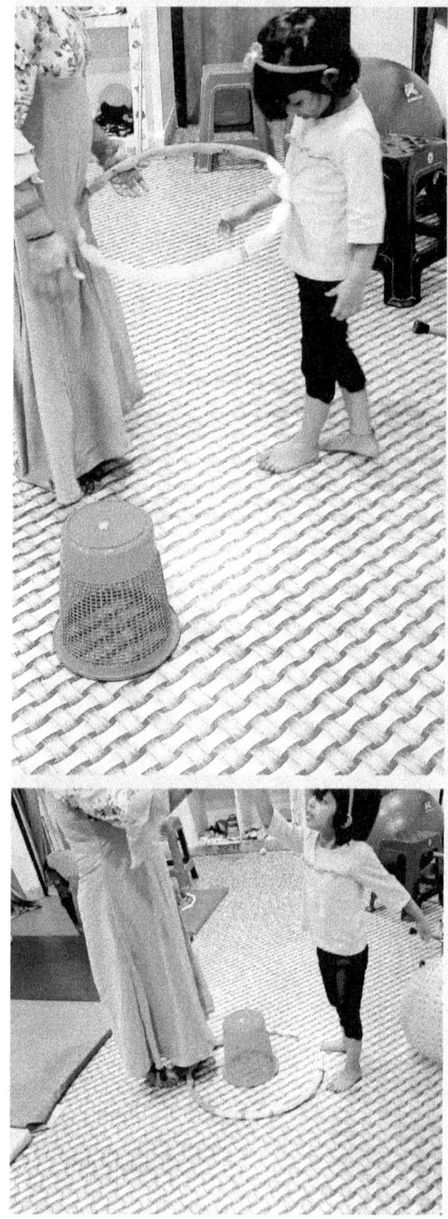

Don't drop the hoop

Don't drop the hoop-

<u>Number of Participants</u> - 2 or more
   <u>Equipment Required</u> –

- Hoola hoops(equal numbers for each team)
- Large cones(one for each team)

<u>How to play</u> –

- Draw a start & finish line using chalk or masking tape at the two ends of a room. Place the large cones at the finish line.
- Make two or three teams each with two participants. Two members of each team stand at the start line holding a hoola hoop with their bellies with their hands behind their back.
- Each team tries to hold the hoola hoop in between their bellies & reach the finish line where they drop the hoola hoop on their cone.
- Then go back to the starting line to get another hoola hoop.
- The team which can drop the maximum number of hoola hoops around the cones wins.

<u>Benefits</u> –
This activity helps in the development of the following skills:

- Following the instructions of the game
- Enjoying games with friends
- Impulse control
- Team work
- Body awareness
- Balance & coordination
- Cooperation
- Competitiveness

- Attention
- Fine motor skills
- Motor planning required to perform the activity
- Sense of accomplishment

• 204 •

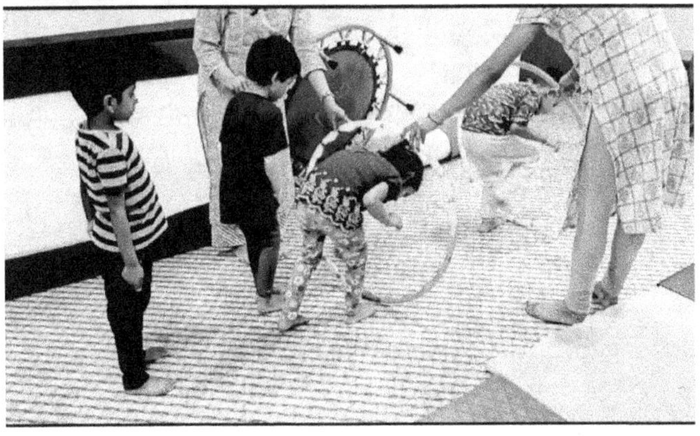

Hoola-Hoop Tunnel

Hoola-Hoop Tunnel -

<u>Number of Participants</u> - 4 or more
    <u>Equipment Required</u> –

- Hoola hoops (atleast 2)
- Puzzles

<u>How to play</u> –

- Two students stand in a line at a little distance from each other. Each student holds a hoola hoop vertically at a height that one kid can bend & go through it like a "caterpillar".
- The two students hold their hoola hoops making a "tunnel" for the "caterpillars" to go through.
- The other two caterpillar take a puzzle placed at one end of the hoola hoop tunnel, go through the tunnels by bending down , crossing the hoop & getting up, again bending down to cross another hoop, & reach the puzzle board placed at the other end of the hoop tunnel.
- Next, change position to hold the hoola hoops while the other two become the "caterpillar."
- Game continues taking turns until all the puzzles are finished.
- For younger kids, teacher can hold the hoola hoops while all the students pass through in a line completing puzzles.

<u>Benefits</u> –
This activity helps in the development of the following skills:

- Following the instructions of the game
- Waiting for your turn in a line
- Impulse control
- Team work

- Motor planning required to perform the activity in a group
- Cooperation
- Body awareness
- Coordinating the timing of entering & moving out of the hoola hoop tunnel with your friends
- Paying attention when it's your turn
- Helping friends

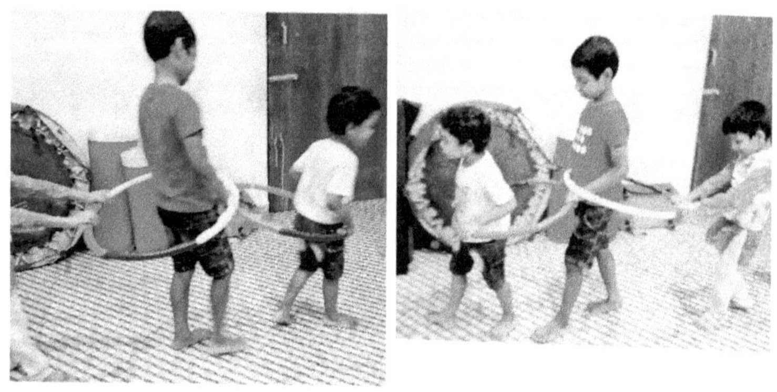

Hoola-Hoop Train

Hoola-Hoop Train-

<u>Number of Participants</u> - 3 or more
   <u>Equipment Required</u> – Hoola hoops
   <u>How to play</u> –

- All the kids stand in a line. There's a hoola-hoop around each child except the last one. The student at the back holds the hoola hoop of the student at the front at his waist level.
- The child at the front is the "Train Driver" who leads all of them.
- You can mark different spots as "Train stops", or "stations". You can either use any object like a large stool, or chair or a box or the door as "Station".
- Make a path for their train- It can be a straight path or with turns.
- When you say "start", the kids all walk in a line holding each other's hoola-hoops with both hands making the "chook chook sound".
- When they arrive at a "Station", they change positions & another child comes to the front. They take turns to change positions at each "station".

  - Alternatively, you can use puzzles to complete. In each round, one student who is the "Train Driver" takes a puzzle & fixes. Then, another student comes to the front & becomes the "Train Driver".
  - Game continues till all puzzles are completed. Make sure each one gets a chance to be the "Train Driver" & others hold each other's hoola hoops while walking.

<u>Benefits</u> –
This game helps in developing the following skills:

- Enjoying with friends
- Team work
- Helping friends
- Bonding with friends

- Following the instructions of the game
- Body awareness required to keep holding their friend's hoola hoop while walking & taking turns
- Motor planning skills
- Impulse control
- Waiting

XVIII

Rope Games

Rope Games (For Older kids)

Hold hands & Jump together

Hold hands & Jump together-

<u>Number of Participants</u> - 2 or more
    <u>Equipment Required</u> –

- A long piece of rope
- Any puzzles

<u>How to play</u> –

- Tie one end of the rope to a window/any other object.
- Mark with a chalk/marker 2 lines one on each side of the rope where the students have to stand. They will jump from that area. The line should not be too far from the rope.
- You can give them puzzles to complete. Put all the puzzle pieces on one side of the rope & the board on the other side.
- Each student picks one puzzle. Then, all stand in a line holding hands on one side of the rope(at the chalk mark)
- The teacher holds one end of the rope & says "1,2,3,jump!"
- All students **jump at a time** to the other side of the rope & fix their puzzles.
- Again they hold hands & stand at the chalk mark. When the teacher says "1,2,3,jump", they jump together to the other side.
- Game continues till all the puzzles are completed.
- The teacher can hold the rope still, or move it slightly in a to-&-fro motion to make the game a little challenging.
- They need to coordinate their jumps in such a manner that all the players jump over the rope **at the same time.**

<u>Benefits</u> –
This activity helps in the development of the following skills:

- Following the instructions of the game
- Body awareness
- Motor planning required to perform the activity
- Listening skills
- Team work
- Bonding with friends
- Helping friends
- Observation & Imitation skills
- Confidence

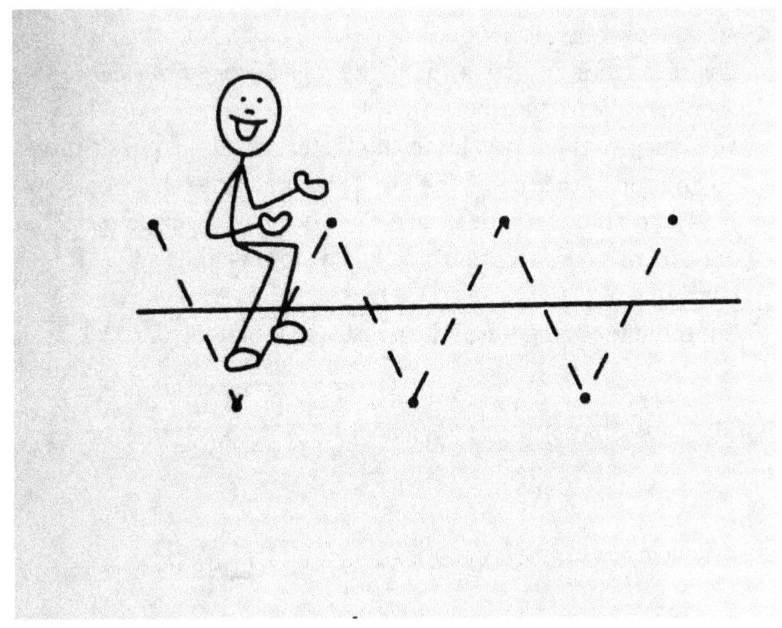

Jump over a stationary rope(side to side)

Jump over a stationary rope-

Number of Participants - 2 or more

<u>Equipment Required</u> –

- A long piece of rope
- Any puzzles

<u>How to play</u> –

- Stretch out the rope in a straight line on the ground. You can also tie the two ends of the rope to any stationary surface(like window/table,etc) so that the rope is at a little height from the ground. Make sure the height is not too much that can't be jumped over by the kids.
- The students start at one end of the rope & ***jump from side to side*** over the rope to the other end.
- You can give them puzzles to complete. Put all the puzzle pieces on one end of the rope & the puzzle board at the other end.
- They can stand in a line, take turns to take a puzzle placed at one end of the rope, jump side to side to the other end & fix the puzzle.
- Continue the game till all the puzzles are completed.

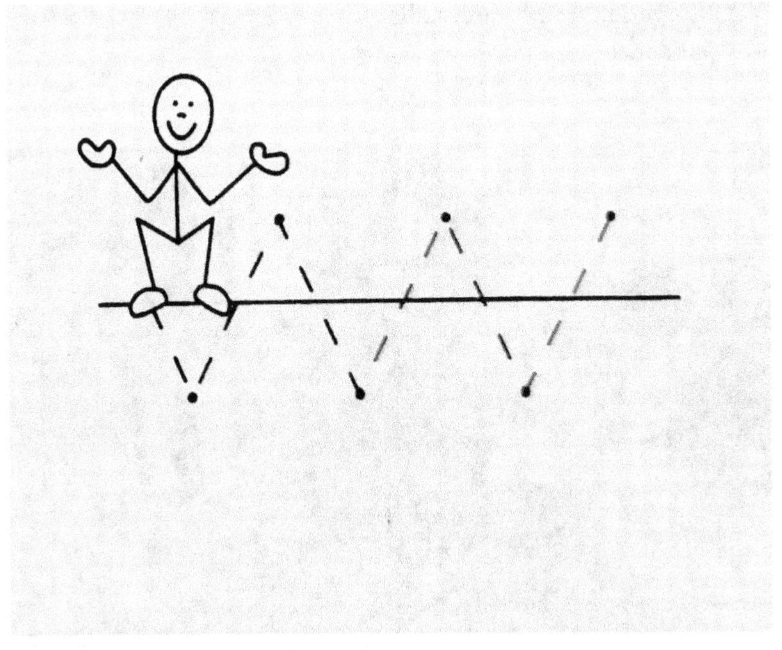

Jump over a stationary rope(forward/backward)

<u>Variation-</u>

- The students can jump forward & backward over the rope & continue down to the end instead of side to side.

<u>Benefits</u> –
This activity helps in the development of the following skills:

- Following the instructions of the game
- Body awareness
- Motor planning required to perform the activity
- Listening skills
- Team work
- Taking turns

- Waiting for your turn
- Observation & Imitation skills
- Confidence

Hold hands & Walk on the Rope

Hold hands & Walk on the Rope-

<u>Number of Participants</u> - 2 or more
<u>Equipment Required</u> –

- A long piece of rope

- Any puzzles

How to play –

- Tie one end of the rope to a window/any other object.
- Place the rope on the floor making any pattern. You can make curves/loops/zig-zag patterns.
- Vary the patterns to make the game easier/difficult for the children.
- You can give them puzzles to complete. Put all the puzzle pieces on one side of the rope & the board on the other side.
- Each student picks one puzzle. Then, all stand in a line holding hands on one end of the rope.
- Now they have to walk along the pattern on the rope holding hands until they reach the puzzle board.
- Fix the puzzles & move along the pattern holding hands again.
- Continue till all the puzzles are completed.

Benefits-
This activity helps in the development of the following skills:

- Following the instructions of the game
- Body awareness
- Motor planning required to perform the activity
- Team work
- Bonding with friends
- Helping friends
- Observation & Imitation skills
- Balance & Coordination

Walk in a Rope

Walk in a Rope

<u>Number of Participants</u> - 3 or more
  <u>Equipment Required</u> –

- A Rope
- Puzzles

<u>How to play</u> –
This game is similar to "walk inside a hoola hoop" except, we are using a ropeinstead of a hoola hoop here.

- All children stand forming a circle inside the rope holding & walk together from one end of the room to the other end completing puzzles.
- Take turns to pick up the puzzle & fix it.
- Others should wait while one kid is fixing a puzzle.
- They all should hold the rope such that it doesn't get slack or fall off.
- Repeat till all puzzles are completed.

<u>Benefits</u> -
This activity helps in the development of the following skills:

- Following the instructions of the game
- Body awareness
- Motor planning required to perform the activity
- Listening skills
- Team work
- Taking turns
- Waiting for your turn
- Observation & Imitation skills
- Confidence

Row row row your boat

Row row row your boat-

<u>Number of Participants</u> - 2 or more
   <u>Equipment Required</u> –

- A long piece of rope

<u>How to play</u> –
You can make teams or take turns with two players in each round. Each team has two players & one rope.

- A pair of children can ***sit, kneel, half-kneel, or stand*** in a line opposite one another.
- Each child grasps a portion of the rope as in a traditional "tug of war". Then, they pull the rope with even pressure & move forward and backward while singing the song "Row row row

your boat".
- They should maintain an even pressure on the rope so that the rope remains taut

- Not with too much pressure to knock down their opponent
- Not with too little pressure that the rope hangs down
<u>Benefits</u> –
This activity helps in the development of the following skills:

- Following the instructions of the game
- Body awareness
- Motor planning required to perform the activity
- Bonding with friends
- Team work
- Impulse Control
- Observation & Imitation skills
- Confidence

Don't touch the rope

Don't touch the rope-

<u>Number of Participants</u> - 4 or more
   <u>Equipment Required</u> –

- A Jump rope

<u>How to play</u> –
Two children hold the rope. The remaining children stand in a line waiting for the teacher's command to start running. You can mark the start & stop lines.

- The children holding the rope start turning it in a consistent rhythmical manner.
- When the teacher commands "start", each student starts running from the starting line towards the rope & runs through/under the rope without letting the rope touch them.
- Take turns & shift positions with the ones holding the rope.

<u>Benefits</u> –
This activity helps in the development of the following skills:

- Enjoying games with friends
- Following the instructions of the game
- Understanding games with rules
- Body awareness
- Motor planning required to perform the activity
- Team work
- Taking turns
- Waiting for your turn
- Observation & Imitation skills
- Confidence

XIX
Ball & Balloon Games

Ball & Balloon Games

Tap the balloon on name call

Tap the balloon on name call-

Number of Participants - 3 or more
    Equipment Required – None
    How to play –

- All the kids sit/stand in a line or a small circle.
- The teacher stands in the front holding the balloon. She/he calls out the name of a student & taps the balloon to him/her. The student quickly taps the balloon to the teacher.
- Each student comes to the front, calls out the name of a friend & taps the balloon towards him.

Benefits –
This game helps in developing the following skills:

- Responding to one's name call
- Waiting for Turn
- Listening skills essential to tap the balloon when "your name is called"
- Remembering your friends' names to tap the balloon.
- Eye contact
- Motor planning skills required to tap the balloon with adequate force & in the direction of his friend
- Attention

Waddle with a Balloon

**Waddle with a Balloon-**

<u>Number of Participants</u> - 2 or more
    <u>Equipment Required</u> –

- Balloons (equal numbers for each participant.)
- Puzzles

<u>How to play</u> –

- Draw a start & finish line using chalk or masking tape at the two ends of a room.
- Each student stands at the starting line with a balloon between their legs. (_As a variation, a ball can be used intead of a balloon_)
- You can give some puzzles for each participant to complete.
- Each student picks up a puzzle, tries to walk by holding the balloon in between his legs & reach the finish line where they fix their puzzles.
- Then go back to get another puzzle.
- You can also set up a small obstacle course that they can cross to make it more challenging & fun.
- Game continues till everyone has completed their puzzles while waddling through the obstacles with a balloon between their legs.

<u>Benefits</u> –
This game helps in developing the following skills:

- Enjoying an activity with friends
- Following instructions of the game
- Bonding with friends
- Motor planning skills
- Body awareness

- Observation & imitation skills
- Impulse control

Pass the Ball-Categories

Pass the Ball-Categories-

<u>Number of Participants</u> - 3 or more

<u>Equipment Required</u> – A ball. (A football or a gymball or a softball can be used)

<u>How to play</u> –

This game is similar to the game of "pass the ball" except you can designate a category name to each participant.

*Example-*Aadi is "Fruit", Som is "Veichle", Kakul is "Vegetables", etc. You can put the same category puzzle board near each kid to help them remember which category they are.

- All the kids sit or stand in a circle at a little distance from one another.
- One child comes to the front.
- Teacher commands- Roll/throw the ball to"Apple". The ball is rolled to Aadi(Fruit)
- Roll or throw the ball to "Car". The ball is rolled to Som(veichle).

<u>Variation for older children</u> –

- The ball can be passed in one bounce, two bounce, etc.

<u>Benefits</u> -

This game helps in developing the following skills:

- Enjoying an activity with friends
- Following instructions of the game
- Bonding with friends
- Cognitive skills
- Listening skills
- Attention
- Observation & imitation skills

- Impulse control
- Waiting for your turn

1,2,3, Throw

1,2,3, Throw-

Number of Participants - 3 or more
  Equipment Required –

- Small balls.

- One bucket/tub

<u>How to play</u> –

- All the kids sit or stand in a line. Use a masking tape or hoola hoops to mark their places.
- One bucket /tub is placed at the front.
- Teacher gives one ball to each kid.
- Then teacher says, "1,2,3,throw!"
- All kids need to throw their balls into the bucket "At the Same time".
- Emphasize the synchronicity of "throwing the balls together" when the teacher says "throw" in this game.

<u>Benefits</u> -

- Enjoying an activity with friends
- Following instructions of the game
- Bonding with friends
- Cognitive skills
- Listening skills
- Team work
- Observation & imitation skills
- Impulse control

Pass the Ball between your legs

Pass the Ball between your legs

<u>Number of Participants</u> - 3 or more
<u>Equipment Required</u> –

- A ball

<u>How to play</u> –
This is a very intresting & fun game.

- All the kids stand in a line at a little distance from one another with wide legs.
- All kids need to stand in a straight line so that when they widen their legs, there's enough space for the ball to be rolled smoothly.
- The student standing at the front starts by rolling a ball in between his legs backwards sending it towards next student standing behind him who again sends it to the student behind him.
- This continues till the ball reaches to the student standing at the last.
- The student standing at the last tries to grab the ball & run towards the front of the line .
- Now, he stands at the front & rolls the ball between his legs towards the back like before.
- Game continues till each student has rolled the ball.

<u>Benefits-</u>

- Enjoying an activity with friends
- Following instructions of the game
- Understanding games with rules
- Bonding with friends
- Cognitive skills
- Team work
- Observation & imitation skills
- Impulse control
- Waiting for your turn

- Motor planning skills required to perform the activity
- Body awareness

XX

Blackboard Games

Blackboard Games (For Older kids)

These games focus mainly upon the skills required for activities in school like-

- Developing the discipline,
- Obervation & imitation skills,
- Standing in a line
- Answering questions
- Writing skills
- Vocabulary
- Spelling
- Imagination & Creativity
- Confidence

Word Game

Word Game-

Number of Participants - 2 or more
   Equipment Required –

- A Blackboard

How to play –

- All students stand in a line. Teacher starts by writing any word on the blackboard.
- The first student writes another word starting with the last letter of the first word written by the teacher.

- Then, the next student writes a word starting with the last letter of the previous word. No word can be repeated twice.
- You can set a timer to see how quickly the participants can remember & write new words.

<u>Benefits</u> –
This activity helps in the development of the following skills:

- Enjoying an activity with friends
- Impulse control
- Taking turns
- Waiting in a line
- Cognitive skills required to follow the rules of the game
- Observation skills
- Attention
- Confidence
- Writing skills
- Learning spellings
- Enhances Vocabulary
- Problem solving skills
- Being organized & focused

Answer the questions - Missing letters

<u>Answer the questions-</u>

<u>Number of Participants</u> - 3 or more
<u>Equipment Required</u> –

- A Blackboard

<u>How to play</u> –

- All students stand in a line.

Teacher can give some -

- Simple additions/subtractions, or,
- Draw small pictures to "Count & write", or,
- Give jumbled words to solve, or,
- Missing letters in some short words

The students can solve their questions turnwise.
<u>Benefits</u> –
This activity helps in the development of the following skills:

- Enjoying an activity with friends
- Impulse control
- Taking turns
- Waiting in a line
- Cognitive skills required to follow the rules of the game
- Observation skills
- Attention
- Confidence
- Writing skills

- Learning spellings, counting, addition/subtractions,etc
- Problem solving skills
- Being organized & focused

Missing Letters

Missing Numbers/Letters-

<u>Number of Participants</u> - 2 or more
   <u>Equipment Required</u> –

- A Blackboard

<u>How to play</u> –

- All students stand in a line.
- Teacher writes 1-50, or, 1-100, sequentially leaving some blanks randomly in between for the students to fill up.
- The students fill up the missing numbers turnwise sequentially.
- They can also fill up "Missing letters" from A-Z in a similar manner turnwise.

<u>Benefits</u> –
This activity helps in the development of the following skills:

- Enjoying an activity with friends
- Taking turns
- Waiting in a line
- Cognitive skills required to follow the rules of the game
- Observation skills
- Attention
- Confidence
- Counting
- Learning sequence of letters & numbers
- Being organized & focused

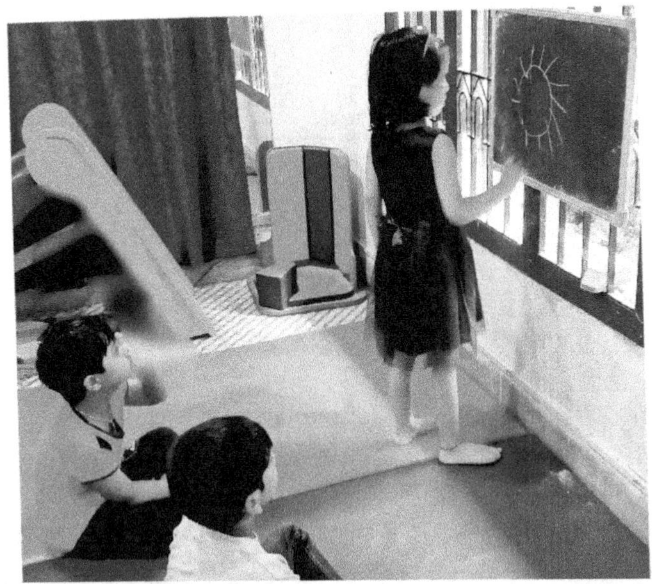

Pictionary

Pictionary-

<u>Number of Participants</u> - 3 or more
    <u>Equipment Required</u> –

- A Blackboard
- Some chits of paper

<u>How to play</u> –

- Make 2-3 teams with atleast two players in each team.
- There are some chits inside a bowl. In each chit, there's a word written. Word can be any common object. Example- A ball
- One member of each team has to draw a picture on the blackboard. The other team members have to guess the word from what he/she has drawn. No talking allowed.
- If they make a correct guess, they get a point.
- You can use the timer, for 1 minute or 2 minutes for each team to guess the word.

<u>Benefits</u> –
This activity helps in the development of the following skills:

- Enjoying an activity with friends
- Cognitive skills to understand the rules of the game
- Team work
- Bonding with friends
- Imagination skills
- Competitiveness
- Observation skills
- Attention
- Confidence

XXI
Clap & Tap Games

Clap & Tap Games

Count & Clap in a sequence

Count & Clap in a sequence-

<u>Number of Participants</u> - 3 or more
   <u>Equipment Required</u> – None
   <u>How to play</u> –

- All the kids sit/stand in a line.
- The teacher stands in the front & starts by clapping once. Next child claps twice. Next kid claps thrice.
- You can continue till 10 claps.

<u>Benefits</u> –
This activity helps in the development of the following skills:

- Enjoying an activity with friends
- Team work
- Listening skills
- Auditory perception skills to listen & count the number of claps the friend before him has clapped
- Cognitive skills required to follow the rules of the game
- Observation skills
- Attention
- Confidence
- Counting
- Being organized & focused

Clap with Me

Clap/Tap with me-

Number of Participants - 3 or more
    Equipment Required – None
    How to play –

- All the kids sit/stand in a line.
- The teacher stands in the front & starts by clapping/tapping in a sequence. The other students copy the same sequence.

Example- Clap twice & one tap once on knee.

- Next, each student comes to the front & claps/taps in a sequence. The other kids copy the same sequence.

<u>Benefits –</u>
This activity helps in the development of the following skills:

- Enjoying an activity with friends
- Cognitive skills required to follow the rules of the game
- Observation & Imitation skills
- Motor planning skills
- Attention
- Confidence
- Counting
- Being organized & focused

Listen & Clap

Listen & Clap-

<u>Number of Participants</u> - 3 or more
    <u>Equipment Required</u> – None
    <u>How to play</u> –

- All the kids sit/stand in a line.
- The teacher stands in the front & gives commands to each student to clap/tap a number of times.
- The students clap/Tap accordingly.
- Next, each student can come front & give commands of clap/tap to his friends.

Example- Two Claps & one tap on knee.
Three times Clap
Two times Clap
<u>Benefits</u> –
This activity helps in the development of the following skills:

- Enjoying an activity with friends
- Listening skills
- Auditory perception skills to listen to, count & clap/tap the number of times asked by the teacher
- Cognitive skills required to follow the rules of the game
- Observation skills
- Attention
- Confidence
- Counting
- Being organized & focused

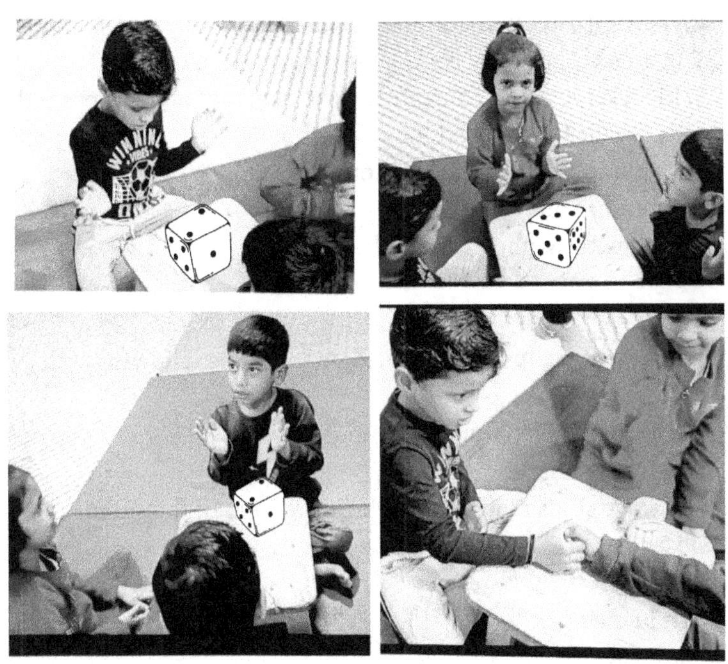

Clap with Dice

Clap with Dice-

<u>Number of Participants</u> - 3 or more
    <u>Equipment Required</u> –

- Ludo Dice

<u>How to play</u> –

This game is similar to "jump with dice" game except for, all participants have to "clap" the number of times that comes.

- All participants stand around a stool/table.
- The first kid starts by rolling the dice on the stool.
- Whichever number comes, he has to clap that many times & then pass the dice to the next kid.
- That kid rolls his dice again, counts the dots & claps according to the number on the dice.
- Continue the game for a few rounds.

Benefits -
This activity helps in the development of the following skills:

- Enjoying an activity with friends
- Listening skills
- Cognitive skills required to follow the rules of the game
- Observation & Imitation skills
- Attention
- Confidence
- Counting
- Being organized & focused

XXII
Traditional Games(with variation)

Traditional Games(with variation)

Hanky Head

Hanky Head-

<u>Number of Participants</u> - 4 or more
 <u>Equipment Required</u> –

- A Hanky

<u>How to play</u> –

- All students sit in a circle close to each other.
- One student is the "Police". He/she has a hanky.
- The "Police" has to run around the back of the circle of students. He slowly drops the hanky on the head of one of the kids.
- Now, that kid becomes the "Police". He has to hold the hanky & start running while the previous "Police" sits at his place.
- If the kid with the hanky doesn't run when the hanky is dropped on him until the police completes one circle around the kids, he/she is out.

<u>Benefits-</u>
This game helps in the development of the following skills-

- Following the instructions of the game
- Understanding games with rules
- Enjoying playing with friends
- Bonding with friends
- Awareness of touch sensation
- Body awareness
- Waiting
- Encouraging friends
- Team work
- Cooperation

Kho-Kho

Kho-Kho-

This game is similar to the above game with a little variation.

    <u>Number of Participants</u> - 4 or more

    <u>Equipment Required</u> –

- None

How to play –

- All students sit in a line in kneeling or half-kneeling position with one facing front & one facing back. They can also sit in cross-legged position if maintaning a kneeling/half-kneeling position is difficult for them.
- One student is the "Police". He/she starts running around the students clockwise.
- He touches one kid at his back saying "Kho"! Whosever back is touched, has to stand & start running while the "Police" will take his place.
- He will now run around the other kids & give "Kho" to another student.
- Game continues for a few rounds. Make sure everyone gets a chance to become the "Police"

Benefits-
This game helps in the development of the following skills-

- Following the instructions of the game
- Understanding games with rules
- Enjoying playing with friends
- Bonding with friends
- Awareness of touch sensation
- Body awareness
- Attention
- Waiting
- Encouraging friends
- Team work
- Cooperation
- Motor planning skills

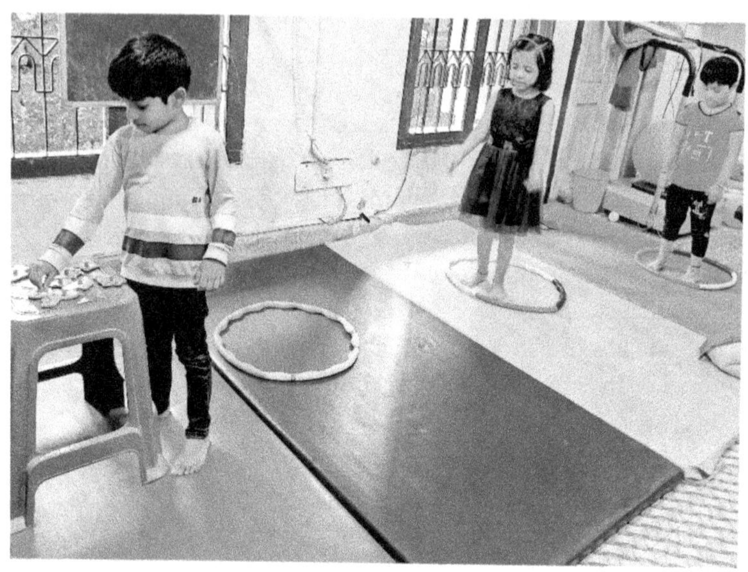

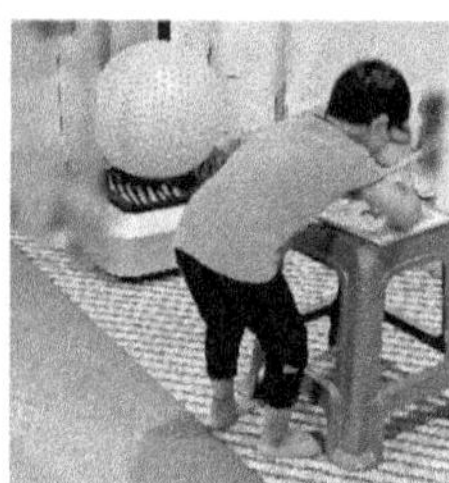

Relay Walk

<u>Relay Walk-</u>

<u>Number of Participants</u> - 3 or more
<u>Equipment Required</u> –

- Puzzles

How to Play-

- You can make two teams each team with atleast two players or, all can play together.
- Place the puzzles at one end & the board at the other end.
- All students stand at a little distance from each other. Use hoola hoops to mark their places.
- Each kid has to pass a puzzle piece to his friend in the hoola hoop & take their place. They keep on passing the puzzle & changing places.
- One kid gets a puzzle, jumps inside the first circle, passes the puzzle to his friend & takes his place. That kid jumps out of his circle & goes to the next circle, passes the puzzle to his friend & takes his place.
- The last kid fixes the puzzle & runs to get another puzzle.
- The game continues till all the puzzles are finished.
- The kids can say "Take it" & "Thank you" while giving the puzzles.

Benefits-
This game helps in the development of the following skills-

- Following the instructions of the game
- Understanding games with rules
- Enjoying playing with friends
- Bonding with friends
- Awareness of touch sensation
- Body awareness
- Attention
- Waiting
- Simple communication skills
- Team work
- Cooperation

Chain Game

Chain Game-

This is another cheerful children's game. This game is more fun to play when there are more players & a large space.

<u>Number of Participants</u> - 4 or more

<u>Equipment Required</u> –

- None

<u>How to Play-</u>

- All kids stand at distance from each other. From among them, a "Denner" is selected.
- When the teacher says "Start", the "Denner" starts chasing his friends to catch.
- The 'denner' has to catch the other members and when the denner catches someone, he joins hands with the denner to form a chain.
- Together they all try to catch or grab the other remaining members and this will go on till all the players have been caught.

<u>Benefits-</u>

This game helps in the development of the following skills-

- Following the instructions of the game
- Enjoying playing with friends
- Bonding with friends
- Awareness of touch sensation
- Body awareness
- Motor planning skills
- Problem solving skills
- Attention
- Encouraging friends

- Team work
- Cooperation
- Confidence
- Leadership

Hide & Seek Game

Hide & Seek Game-

Children really enjoy the age old game of hide & seek. You can easily play inside the house. You can also add some rules for safety. *Example-* No hiding in the kitchen

<u>Number of Participants</u> - 4 or more

<u>Equipment Required</u> –

- None

<u>How to Play-</u>

- All kids stand at distance from each other. From among them, a "Denner" is selected.
- The "Denner" closes his eyes & starts counting 1-50. In the meantime, everyone else has to find a place to hide.
- After counting till 50, The 'denner' has to start searching the members inside the house.
- When the denner catches someone, he joins hands with the denner to search the other members.
- Together they all try to find the other remaining members and this will go on till all the players have been caught.
- Now, the one who is caught at last becomes the "Denner" & the game continues.

<u>Benefits-</u>
This game helps in the development of the following skills-

- Following the instructions of the game
- Understanding games with rules
- Enjoying playing with friends
- Bonding with friends
- Attention
- Waiting
- Team work
- Cognitive skills
- Impulse control

XXIII

Some Real-life stories

"The most interesting people you'll find are ones that don't fit into your average cardboard box. They'll make what they need, they'll make their own boxes." -Dr. Temple Grandin

Our little Stars

I would share a little story that happened recently in my session that will exemplify the message above.

It was a group class that day. There were about 5 students. They were given some pictures to colour. The objective was to teach cooperation, sharing, & communication of one's needs while enjoying the colouring activity. Among those students, there was a kid who was not paying any attention to the activity or to what I was saying. She was repeatedly making some sounds & everyone else was getting distracted because of those sounds she was making. I got a little annoyed with her. Only one student- Saima completed the colouring activity beautifully & attentively that day. I was really happy with Saima's painting.

So, I decided to give a star on her painting as a reward. When I was giving her the "star" telling everyone how beautiful her painting is, She took another kid's painting, gave it to me & asked- "Ma'am give a star", then she took everyone else's painting too one by one & asked me to give a star to everyone! Although I was a bit reluctant at first that I should give the star "only to the one with the best painting/only to the deserving one", this sweet act of hers, melted my heart. It was her way of saying- "We all are Stars! No terms & conditions!" I gave a star to each one of them & there was a big smile on their faces. The student who was disturbing everyone making sounds also stopped making sounds & started participating nicely & enjoying all other activities with her friends that day! They were all happy. This sweet gesture of hers helped each one of them to learn valuing friendship, connection, helping each other & loving unconditionally. Not just the students, but I was also more at ease & became more focused on having a good time with the students. I understood something important that day...

"Children will learn the essence of communication, sharing, friendship, socialization when they are having fun way more than by following the rules & doing things exactly the way they need to be done."

That incident is a great example of "The joy, satisfaction & reward of Loving unconditionally" taught by a child!

Along with that, through this game, the children learnt some important life skills of-

- Cooperation
- Sharing
- Communicating their needs, as well as understanding the needs of others
- Valuing friendship
- Enjoying an activity together
- Focusing on completing their activity

Success stories

I have already mentioned the numerous benefits of group games earlier in chapter 2. Participating in group games has brought a lot of positive changes in children.

Gundu, used to push other kids at times(which was her form of interaction with other kids). Although she didn't mean to hurt anyone, this had created a negative impact on her friends at school. Now, she has stopped pushing others. Instead, she has become very sociable with others. Also, she has stopped pushing other kids both at school & other places. She tries to communicate with other kids instead of pushing.

Kakul, used to be very very shy at school & with any new person. She didn't know how to interact with other kids & thus was very reluctant to go to school & avoided interaction with other kids. She preffered to be alone most of the time. Now, she loves to be around other kids. She wants to participate in different group activities at school, at home, therapy centres & everywhere else. She even has started interacting with them & enjoys in group. She is no longer uncomfortable even with new teachers or other adults & relatives. Recently, in a sports competition, she had won the 2nd prize in running competition in her school! She also got the maximum participation award for participating in all the events that were organized that day. It was a tremendous achievement for her.

Aadi, due to sensory issues used to avoid being touched by other kids & teachers he is unfamiliar with. He preferred to play alone mostly. Now, he takes an inetrest in group activities for his favorite games. He tries to interact with his friends, follows commands in a group nicely, participates in games with rules, remembers his friends' names, communicates his needs in therapy centre, & at school also.

Shivya, used to run around in between class time as she needed movement breaks & it's difficult for her to sit still for long especially in classroom where there is a bombardment of sensory information. She also couldn't interact & socialize with her friends. Now, she is socializing really well in group sessions, interacting with all her friends. She has also started to sit in her class in school & is much more attentive to the teacher, even answers questions with confidence. She has also developed the sense of competitiveness at therapy sessions & at school also & is participating in any game/ activity with passion & dedication.

Khush, who although was good academically & listened to his teachers, had difficulty making friends, interacting with them, or enjoying games with friends. Now, he has started enjoying with friends, started interacting with his friends, & bonding with them in the therapy sessions & at school also.

"Playing in groups has not only helped these children to develop some important life skills, it also has helped to instill some beautiful values within them like- being kind to others, uplifting & encouraging others when they are down, helping someone in need, accepting & enjoying with different people with different skill levels, working with others, & to keep getting up after falling, to keep trying again next time..."

"It's the things we play with and the people who help us play that make a great difference in our lives.
Fred Rogers"

BOOK SUMMARY

Play is the basis of almost all learning in early childhood & afterwards also.

Babies explore their environment and make sense of new and different information by engaging in play. **The experiences babies have during play help strengthen and expand networks of connections in their developing brains**. During the early years, babies' brains form many more connections than the brain will ever need. Research has shown that when a child enjoys doing something, the ability to learn & retain what he has learned is much much more than when it's not enjoyable/needs a lot of effort. *This rule applies to learning anything- be it life skills like, making friends, socialization, interaction with others, problem solving skills, decison making skills, leadership skills, etc, or academic skills.*

Both structured & unstructured play are crucial in the development of gross motor, fine motor, social, emotional, communication & life skills from a young age.

The list of 100 games mentioned in this book are simple & fun structured games focusing on the development & mastering of all these skills in children. They have been categorized into different types to make it easier for the readers to choose & implement them based on which areas you want to focus upon. You will get a good variety of games to practice different skills in children.

We have practiced these games with many children & they have proved to be very effective in developing & strengthening all of these skills within a very short period of time. Be it a child with special need or a normal child, the lessons & values that they have & are learning through these games will help them become confident, kind, creative, smart, inspiring & sociable person.

"Play is often talked about as if it was a relief from serious learning, but for children, play is serious learning. Play is really the work of childhood.

Fred Rogers"

About The Author

About the Author

The writer's name is Abhipsa Parida. She is an occupational therapist with a specialisation in developmental disabilities. She has been handling children with special needs since the last 7 years. She has done her Bachelor as well as Masters in Occupational therapy from SVNIRTAR, Olatpur. She is quite experienced and skillful in observation, assessment and planning intervention for children with special needs. She has worked in various Occupational therapy centres for children with special needs and has handled many kids of different age groups with varying needs. At present, she is successfully running her own therapy centre in Bhubaneswar.

Along with that, she is also a blogger who has published a number of articles on different common problems faced by children with special needs & ways to handle them. She also has a youtube channel- **OT FOR KIDS by Abhipsa Parida** in which she has posted some very useful videos for children with special needs.

You can check out her articles at - **abhipsaot.blogspot.com**

She is also the author of the book – **"BEING JOYFUL WITH AUTISM" (available in Amazon/Flipkart/Notionpress)** which is very much appreciated & acknowledged by many parents of children with special needs & proffessionals. She also has been awarded with the **"AUTHORITY AWARD"** by the Indian Institute of Health Sciences for her remarkable contribution in this field.

If you have any queries, you can mail them at abhipsaot21@gmail.

www.ingramcontent.com/pod-product-compliance
Lightning Source LLC
Chambersburg PA
CBHW072211150726
48002CB00005B/1756